Jewish Exiles' Psychological Interpretations of Nazism

"Accurate scholarship can
Unearth the whole offence
From Luther until now
That has driven culture mad,
Find what occurred at Linz [where Hitler was raised],
What huge imago made
A psychopathic god:
I and the public know
What all schoolchildren learn,
Those to whom evil is done
Do evil in return."
—W. H. Auden, "September 1, 1939"

Avihu Zakai

Jewish Exiles' Psychological Interpretations of Nazism

palgrave
macmillan

Avihu Zakai
Department of History
The Hebrew University of Jerusalem
Jerusalem, Israel

ISBN 978-3-030-54069-2 ISBN 978-3-030-54070-8 (eBook)
https://doi.org/10.1007/978-3-030-54070-8

Cover illustration: Cole Carothers / Alamy Stock Photo. Pictured on cover are Wilhelm Reich, Erich Fromm, Siegfried Kracauer, and Erich Neumann.

This Palgrave Macmillan imprint is published by the registered company Springer Nature Switzerland AG.
The registered company address is: Gewerbestrasse 11, 6330 Cham, Switzerland

Contents

Introduction

Jewish Exiles' Psychological Interpretations of Nazism examines works of four German-Jewish scholars who, in their places of exile, sought to probe the pathology of the Nazi mind: Wilhelm Reich's *The Mass Psychology of Fascism* (1933), Erich Fromm's *Escape from Freedom* (1941), Siegfried Kracauer's *From Caligari to Hitler: A Psychological History of the German Film* (1947), and Erich Neumann's *Depth Psychology and a New Ethic* (1949). While scholars have examined these authors' individual legacies, no comparative analysis of their shared concerns has yet been undertaken, nor have the content and form of their psychological inquiry into Nazism been seriously and systematically analyzed. Yet, the sense of urgency in their works calls for attention. They all took up their pens to counter Nazi barbarism, believing, like the English jurist and judge Sir William Blackstone, that "*scribere est agere*" (to write is to act).[1]

The works discussed in the present study formed part of a well-defined grand *Kulturkampf* leveled against Nazi and Fascist barbarism and totalitarianism by exiled intellectuals from Nazi Europe, which profoundly transformed the content and form of modern intellectual history. The list is impressive: Max Horkheimer and Theodore Adorno, *Dialectic of Enlightenment* (1944, revised 1947) and Horkheimer, *Eclipse of Reason* (1947); Franz Leopold Neumann, *Behemoth: The Structure and Practice of National Socialism, 1933–1944* (1944); Karl Popper, *The Open Society and*

[1] *The Oxford Edition of Blackstone's Commentaries on the Laws of England; Book 4: Of Public Wrongs* (Oxford: Oxford University Press, 2016), 53.

A. Zakai, *Jewish Exiles' Psychological Interpretations of Nazism*,
https://doi.org/10.1007/978-3-030-54070-8_1

Its Enemies (1945); Ernst Cassirer, *The Myth of the State* (1946); Erich Auerbach, *Mimesis: The Representation of Reality in Western Literature* (1946); Thomas Mann, *Doktor Faustus* (1947); Siegfried Kracauer, *From Caligari to Hitler: A Psychological History of the German Film* (1947); Erich Neumann, *Depth Psychology and a New Ethic* (*Tiefenpsychologie und Neue Ethik;* 1949); Hannah Arendt, *The Origins of Totalitarianism* (1951); Leo Strauss, *Natural Right and History* (1953); Hans Baron, *The Crisis of the Early Italian Renaissance* (1966), among many others.[2] The constant point of reference they shared was Nazism, which they analyze and contest with the disciplinary weapons they had honed over a lifetime. It is only within this broad intellectual and historical context, I argue, that the four psychological studies of Nazism considered here acquire their full meaning and significance.

Along with other political, social, historical and sociological interpretations of Nazism written by intellectual exiles from Nazi Germany, such as Horkheimer and Adorno's *Dialectic of Enlightenment* (1944) and Auerbach's *Mimesis: The Representation of Reality in Western Literature* (1946), the four works I analyze here explore the powerful psychological lure of Fascism and Nazism and the evolution of totalitarian and authoritarian states and societies.

In their influential *Anti-Oedipus* (1972), the French philosopher Gilles Deleuze and French psychoanalyst Félix Guattari commended the Austrian Wilhelm Reich for discovering "[w]hy individuals fight *for* their servitude as stubbornly as though it promised their salvation."[3] They argued that Reich is at his most profound when he rejects the explanation of Fascism that rests on the masses' ignorance or delusions, focusing instead on their frustrations and desires. Fromm similarly argued that since humanity cannot live with the dangers and responsibilities inherent to freedom, it invariably turns to authoritarianism. Deploying the insights of psychoanalysis, Fromm finds the pathology of contemporary civilization in its willingness to submit to totalitarian rule, declaring that "the

[2] Some of these works have recently been analyzed in the following publications: Avihu Zakai, *Erich Auerbach and the Crisis of German Philology: The Humanist Tradition in Peril* (Dordrecht: Springer, 2017); David Weinstein and Avihu Zakai, *Jewish Exiles and European Thought in the Shadow of the Third Reich: Baron, Popper, Strauss, Auerbach* (Cambridge: Cambridge University Press, 2017); and Zakai, *The Pen Confronts the Sword: Exiled German Scholars Challenge Nazism* (Albany: SUNY, 2018).

[3] Deleuze and Guattari, *Anti-Oedipus: Capitalism and Schizophrenia* (1972; rpt. London: Continuum, 2004), p. 29; emphasis original.

understanding of the reasons for the totalitarian flight from freedom is a premise for any action which aims at the victory over the totalitarian forces."[4] Kracauer's study proposes a link between the apolitical and "escapist" orientation of Weimar-era cinema and Germany's consequent turn to totalitarianism. These films, he maintains, reflected "society's state of paralysis," "ignored social reality," and revealed an "escapist tendency."[5] Kracauer broke new ground in exploring the connections between film aesthetics, the prevailing psychological *Stimmung* of Weimar Germany, and the evolving social and political Fascism. Finally, Neumann argued that the modern world bears witness to a radical eruption of the dark, negative forces of human nature. The "old ethic," an illusory quest for "perfection" by repressing our "dark side," could no longer deal with contemporary problems. He was convinced that the deadliest peril confronting humanity was the "scapegoat" psychology inherent in the old ethic. We succumb to the grip of this psychology when we project our own "dark shadow" onto an individual or group identified as our "enemy."[6] This tendency led to the mass murder of human beings in Nazi concentration and labor camps.

Taken as a whole, these different psychological interpretations provide important insights into the unique psychological phenomenon of Nazism and the dialectic that engenders authoritarian tendencies. They furthermore elucidate the trauma of Nazism. Trauma inevitably scars the texts it spawns, and this unprecedented social and political trauma scarred these thinkers deeply – however skillfully they buried their scars beneath layers of erudition to compose a wide-ranging defense of western civilization that would outlast the "thousand-year Reich."

Chapter, "Wilhelm Reich and the Sexual Roots of Fascism," addresses the work of Wilhelm Reich (1897–1957), the Austrian physician and psychoanalyst, who belonged to the generation of analysts that succeeded Freud. He penned several influential books, most notably *Character Analysis* (1933), which served for many years as an excellent introduction to psychoanalytic technique; *The Mass Psychology of Fascism* (1933), in which he explained the rise of Fascism as a symptom of sexual repression,

[4] Fromm, *Escape from Freedom* (New York: Rinehart & Company, 1941), viii.

[5] Siegfried Kracauer, *From Caligari to Hitler: A Psychological History of the German Film* (1947; Princeton: Princeton University Press, 2004), pp. 139–40.

[6] Neumann, *Depth Psychology and a New Ethic* (London: Hodder and Stoughton, 1969 [1949]), back cover.

a particular instance of "the social function of sexual repression;"[7] and *The Sexual Revolution* (1936), which analyzes the crisis of bourgeois sexual morality and the failure of sexual reforms that merely preserved the frame of capitalist society. By virtue of the latter two works, Reich became known as one of the most radical figures in the history of psychiatry. Along with Erich Fromm and Herbert Marcuse, Reich emphasized the close connection between psychology and Marxism, but he was the first to offer a psychological interpretation of Fascism and Nazism (Fromm's *Fear of Freedom* appeared in 1942).

In Nazi and Fascist ideology, Reich believed, a repressive family, a baneful religion, a sadistic educational system, party terrorism, fear of economic manipulation, fear of racial contamination, and sanctioned violence against minorities all operated in and through individuals' collective unconscious psychology of emotions, traumatic experiences, fantasies, and libidinal economies. Nazi political ideology and practice exacerbated and exploited these tendencies. Later in life, Reich became a very controversial figure as his message of sexual liberation perturbed the psychoanalytic community and violated the key taboos of psychoanalysis.

Reich's writings influenced generations of intellectuals and he served as midwife for the "sexual revolution." During the 1968 uprisings in Paris and Berlin, students scrawled his name on walls and hurled copies of *The Mass Psychology of Fascism* at police. The French philosopher Gilles Deleuze and psychoanalyst Félix Guattari commended him in their influential *Anti-Oedipus* (1972), claiming that Reich was "at his profoundest as a thinker when he refuses to accept ignorance or illusion on the part of the masses as an explanation of fascism, and demands an explanation that will take their desires into account, an explanation formulated in terms of desire." "The masses were not innocent dupes," he argued, "under a certain set of conditions, they *wanted* fascism, and it is this perversion of the desire of the masses that needs to be accounted for."[8]

Chapter, "A Psychological Inquiry into Totalitarianism: Erich Fromm's *Escape from Freedom*," explores Erich Fromm's *Escape from Freedom* (1941), which charts the growth and decline of freedom and self-awareness in the West from the Middle Ages to modern times, when people sought refuge from insecurity and responsibility in totalitarian movements such as

[7] Reich, *The Mass Psychology of Fascism* (1933; rpt. New York: Farrar, Straus & Giroux, 1970), pp. 24–25.

[8] Deleuze and Guattari, *Anti-Oedipus*, p. 29; emphasis original.

Nazism and Fascism. The rupture of the traditional religious and class bonds of medieval society, Fromm believed, sparked a new independence as well as an anxious alienation that ultimately drove robotic conformity and submission to authority. Fromm explicitly sought to address "the cultural and social crisis of our day," namely Fascism and Nazism.[9]

Contrary to the thesis that Lawrence Friedman expounds in his *The Lives of Erich Fromm: Love's Prophet* (2013), in which he asserts that *Escape from Freedom* demonstrates "the Americanization of a European intellectual," Fromm saw freedom, or the lack of it, as an acute problem rather in Nazi Germany, not in America. Likewise, Popper's *The Open Society and Its Enemies* offered an uncompromising defense of liberal democracy not because it was lacking in New Zealand or England or America, but rather in response to the intellectual origins of totalitarianism in Germany. Cassirer wrote *The Myth of the State* not because the political mode of historical thought it addresses prevailed in America, but rather to show how primitive myths prepared the ground for the rise of the modern totalitarian state in Germany. Arendt did not write *The Origins of Totalitarianism* because it infected America, but sought, rather, to portray and analyze Nazism and Stalinism, the major political movements of the first half of the twentieth century in Europe. In short, the members of this distinguished group of German-speaking intellectual exiles were, in Walt Whitman's words, "language-shapers on other shores."[10] Their language and concepts were formed and fused amid the crucial ideological and intellectual struggles of a specific, wretched moment in German history – the rise and triumph of Nazism; hence, all these thinkers waged a *Kulturkampf* against Nazi barbarism in a bid to save Western humanism and civilization.

Chapter, "Siegfried Kracauer's *From Caligari to Hitler:* Weimar Cinema as Pandora's Box," analyses *From Caligari to Hitler: A Psychological History of the German Film* (1947), in which Siegfried Kracauer (1889–1966) argued that the Weimar screen mirrored the profound trauma of defeat in World War I. It exposed the naked German soul, flailing between tyranny and chaos, and eventually lumbering toward the rise and triumph of Nazism. Kracauer maintained that "through an analysis of the German films deep psychological dispositions predominant in Germany

[9] Fromm, *Escape from Freedom* (New York: Rinehart & Company, 1941), vii–viii.

[10] Walt Whitman, *Leaves of Grass*, ed. W. Blodgett and S. Bradley (New York: New York University Press, 1965), 18.

from 1918 to 1933 can be exposed – dispositions which influenced the course of events and which will have to be reckoned with in the post-Hitler era."[11] Kracauer's study takes the form of an inquiry into the inner workings of the psychological history not only of the German film but of the Weimar Republic itself. It presents its argument in four well-defined acts: the Archaic Period (1895–1918), when a national cinema began to emerge; the Postwar Period (1918–1924), when diabolical characters portended surrender to the irrational; the Stabilized Period (1924–1929), in which a paralyzed German society was unable to resolve its problems; and the Pre-Hitler Period (1929–1933), marked by unmistakable signs of the widespread despair that paved the way for the Nazi revolution and the Nazi state.

Evil and hell are familiar literary tropes that serve various purposes. The first half of Homer's *Odyssey* and the first part of Virgil's *Aeneid* end with an unsettling visit to the underworld. Dante consigned many of his Florentine enemies to the *Inferno*, from which Virgil safely guides him; in *Ignatius His Conclave* (1611), John Donne placed Ignatius Loyola and others he deemed enemies of the true Christian faith in hell. For these writers, hell was elsewhere. By contrast, Kracauer points to the Weimar movies to show how satanic and demonic elements were ingrained in the German imagination: hell is here. He argued that characters and events portrayed in the Weimar movies "now came true in life itself" in the Nazi state, as dreadful apparitions "walked about in the flesh."[12]

A broad array of evil characters and apparitions walk among us, nullify our shame and responsibility, and drive us down a straight and narrow path through social chaos. Before Thomas Mann configured the Nazi state and concentration camps as hell in *Doctor Faustus*, Kracauer discovered a latent diabolic strain in the German soul that emerged after World War I. The Weimar films presaged the coming of the Nazi state's hell on earth. They were reminiscent of Pandora's box—out of which flew a multitude of unforeseen evils and travails—and as in Greek tragedy, prophetic visions of doom and calamity announced in the first act came to their horrifying, devastating culmination in the final act, the Nazi state.

Moreover, while Virgil's *Aeneid*, Dante's *Divine Comedy*, and Milton's *Paradise Regained* all celebrate the ultimate triumphant victory of good

[11] Siegfried Kracauer, *From Caligari to Hitler: A Psychological History of the German Film* (1947; Princeton: Princeton University Press, 2004), li.

[12] Ibid., p. 272.

over evil, the works of Kracauer and Mann lay out a path toward devastating failure. Terrible omens lead to doom and destruction: the fall of the Weimar Republic in Kracauer's rendering and the destruction of the Nazi state in Mann's. In both, frightening portents discernible in the German history of their own times boded impending evil. *From Caligari to Hitler* may well be seen as a prolog to *Doctor Faustus*; for Kracauer, the somnambulist manipulated by the evil hypnotist Caligari and Weimar Germany are one; the Nazi horror and terror "was as it had been on the screen. *The dark premonitions of final doom were also fulfilled.*"[13] As for Mann, the devil who manipulates his Doctor Faustus and Germany are one. Mann's apocalyptic reading of German history traces a path from "Luther and the Reformation to the smoking ruins of the German cities and the gates of the concentration camps."[14] Both authors observe Fascism and Nazism within the broader context of an imminent eschatology and apocalypse hovering above German history.

Chapter, "Erich Neumann and the Western Crisis of Ethics," explores Erich Neumann's *Depth Psychology and a New Ethic* (*Tiefenpsychologie und Neue Ethik*, 1949), which he began to write nine years after leaving Nazi Germany for Palestine in 1934. During the 1930s, he spent most of his time working on *The Origins and History of Jewish Consciousness*, a two-volume study (published in 1949). Now, in 1942, he was living in Tel Aviv when the news came that *Panzerarmee Afrika* under Field Marshal Erwin Rommel had started the second phase of its advance toward Egypt, aiming to seize the oilfields all the way to the Caspian Sea. Already aware of the Holocaust, the small groups of Jewish settlers in Palestine could only expect the worst. At this crucial existential moment, with Rommel "at the door," as Neumann put it, he began writing *Depth Psychology* to reveal the psychological antecedents of the triumph of Nazism and the horrors of the Second World War.

Depth Psychology refers to therapeutic approaches that explore the subtle unconscious and transpersonal aspects of human experience, including dreams, complexes, and archetypes. Neumann sought to offer a psychological interpretation of the vicissitudes of his time and history, the "Age

[13] Ibid., p. 272; emphasis added.

[14] Todd Kontje, *Thomas Mann's World: Empire, Race, and the Jewish Question* (Ann Arbor: University of Michigan Press, 2011), p. 153.

of Catastrophe" in Eric Hobsbawm's words.[15] In a letter to Jung he claimed that his book "was an attempt to process a series of phantasies that roughly corresponded timewise with *the extermination of the Jews*, and in which the problem of evil and justice was being tossed around me."[16] Neumann deployed Jungian concepts at the heart of his book, especially the archetype of the "shadow," denoting the animal side of our personality, which he conceived as the source of twentieth-century brutality and upheaval. The "old" Judeo-Christian ethic had pursued an impossible perfection by repressing the shadow; hence, it had lost its power to negotiate modern Western ambiguities and was blown away. For Neumann, "the old concept of sin has become untrue, it is no longer effective, and that is not due to the decline of man but to his new understanding of himself and God."[17]

Neumann reflects on human destructiveness and the way the human mind relates to its own shadow, to the savage aspect of our personality: "The modern world has witnessed a dramatic breakthrough of the dark, negative forces of human nature. The 'old ethic,' which pursued an illusory perfection by repressing the dark side, has lost its power to deal with contemporary problems … the deadliest peril now confronting humanity lay in the 'scapegoat' psychology associated with the old ethic."[18] Suppression or repression of the shadow produces hostile reactions, which disturb the life of the entire community and keep it in a state of constant unrest. The scapegoat psychology associated with the old ethic makes the most disastrous impact on the life of the collective, leading to wars and the extermination of groups that question the opinions of the majority. Under the pretext of upholding morality in the face of evil, this psychological orientation prompts campaigns of annihilation against neighbors. More specifically, asserted Neumann, wars are a corollary of the old ethic, and warfare is the visible manifestation of the breakthrough of the collective's unconscious shadowy side.[19] The only way to avoid the disastrous consequences of projecting this shadow onto others was to recognize its true origin and integrate it with the totality of the self.

[15] Eric Hobsbawm. *The Age of Extremes: The Short Twentieth Century, 1914–1991* (New York: Pantheon, 1994), 6–7.

[16] Neumann to Jung, June 14, 1957, in *Analytical Psychology in Exile*, 331, emphasis added.

[17] Ibid., 333.

[18] Erich Neumann, *Depth Psychology and a New Ethic*, back cover.

[19] Ibid., p. 58.

According to Neumann's "new ethic," we must all accept the evil within us. Rather than seeking to cast it out or repress it, we should suffer it, sometimes act it out, and pay the price in sorrow and guilt. Neumann therefore envisioned a new human condition based on consciousness as well as the collective unconscious, which accepts darkness and negativity. He cast the shadow shared by all across the divide between perceptions of who is good or evil that plague modern history. Like a Copernican revolution, depth psychology gazed at the shadow to find the true origin of light. It discovered the universal essence and structure of human nature, thereby laying the foundation for a new human solidarity or brotherhood of man amid the ruins of the Second World War. Acknowledging the shadow as its common dimension, humanity has no option but to huddle closer together. The book thus ultimately strove to overcome the awful course of modern history by offering a "new ethic" that would serve as the basis for a new human solidarity.

Wilhelm Reich and the Sexual Roots of Fascism

The Mass Psychology of Fascism (1933) was the first psychological inquiry into Fascism. In this work the psychoanalyst Wilhelm Reich (1897–1957) explores how Fascists came into power, and explain their rise as a symptom of sexual repression. It was followed by other psychological interpretations of Nazism by Jewish exiles from the Third Reich, from Erich Fromm's *Escape from Freedom* (1942), to Siegfried Kracauer's *From Caligari to Hitler: A Psychological History of the German Film* (1947), and Erich Neumann's *Depth Psychology and a New Ethic* (1949).

Introduction

> Indeed, sex-economy goes so far as to say that the abominable excesses of the capitalist era of the past three thousand years … were possible only because the human structure of the untold masses who had endured all this had become totally dependent upon authority, incapable of freedom and extremely accessible to mysticism. (Reich, *The Mass Psychology of Fascism* (p. xxvii))

The iconoclastic Marxist Freudian psychiatrist Wilhelm Reich (1897–1957) developed a system of psychoanalysis that focused on overall character structures rather than individual neurotic symptoms. He argued that aggressive and destructive behavior derives from inhibited urges; that consciousness constitutes only a small part of psychic life; that libido, or sexual desire, is its prime motor; and that childhood fear of parental retribution

A. Zakai, *Jewish Exiles' Psychological Interpretations of Nazism*,
https://doi.org/10.1007/978-3-030-54070-8_2

for perceived sexual transgression festers into severe unconscious conflicts with serious consequences.

Like the German-American philosopher, sociologist, and political theorist Herbert Marcuse (1898–1979) and the Hungarian psychoanalyst and anthropologist Géza Róheim (1891–1953), Reich belonged to "the Freudian Left." The members of this circle were convinced of the unparalleled power of sex in both individual psychology and the evolution of society. They all asserted that sexual pleasure is the ultimate measure of human happiness and hence denounced the sexual repressiveness of modern civilization.[1] Early in his professional career, Reich attempted to synthesize his psychological and political commitments. For example, as a member of the Austrian Social Democratic Party between 1927 and 1930, he helped to establish six socialist sex-hygiene clinics, which provided psychoanalytic counseling in the Vienna area. These clinics proved very popular, rousing party leaders' fears that they were "sapping … energy from the political and economic struggle. As a result, they were closed down in 1930."[2] Reich set up further clinics when he moved to Berlin that same year and joined the Communist Party. The German Association for Proletarian Sexual Politics was formed in Berlin and acquired a membership of over 40.000.[3]

Reich published several influential books on psychoanalytic technique: *The Function of Orgasm* (1927), *Character Analysis* (1933), and *The Mass Psychology of Fascism* (1933). However, his involvement in the sexual politics movement overshadowed his works. He developed a pseudoscientific system he called "orgonomy"—a conflation of *orgasm* and *organism*—based on a biological energy he claimed to have discovered in 1939 and that others called God. Orgone, Reich believed, was "the currency of the cosmos, physically measurable,"[4] a substantive *élan vital* (vital impetus).

In *The Function of Orgasm* (*Die Funktion des Orgasmus*, 1927), Reich argued that the ability to achieve orgasm, called *orgastic potency*, is an essential attribute of the healthy individual; failure to dissipate pent-up sexual energy by orgasm could produce neurosis in adults. His theory of orgastic potency, "the key to both personal and collective health,"

[1] Paul A. Robinson, *The Freudian Left: Wilhelm Reich, Géza Róheim, Herbert Marcuse* (New York: Harper Colophon Books, 1969), pp. 4–5.

[2] Ibid., pp. 39–40.

[3] Jerome Greenfield, *Wilhelm Reich vs. the USA* (New York: Norton, 1974), p. 26.

[4] David Bennett, *The Currency of Desire: Libidinal Economy, Psychoanalysis and Sexual Revolution* (London: Lawrence & Wishart, 2016), p. 136.

construed "orgasm as a universal, natural right" that "a genuinely egalitarian society" should protect. Conversely, "sex-economy theory" or "libidinal thrift produced neurosis at best, cancer and fascism, at worst."[5] Reich's concept of psychic energy is materialistic and mechanistic, opposed to any spiritualization of sexuality. Neurotics, he believed, fall ill because they are unable to achieve a satisfactory orgasm; he equated genital satisfaction with psychic and physical health. *The Function of Orgasm* gave rise to the sexual politics movement, which added advocacy of sexual education and freedom to radical left-wing politics. In the end, Reich believed that the object of psychoanalytic therapy was "the establishment of orgastic potency."[6] He dedicated *The Function of Orgasm* to Freud, yet the reaction of the Father of Psychoanalysis was lukewarm and half-hearted at best.

Reich's *Character Analysis* (*Charakteranalyse*, 1933) presented his teachings on psychoanalytic technique, which "were crucial to his whole group of contemporaries"[7] and contributed to the development of Anna Freud's *The Ego and the Mechanisms of Defence* (1936). His idea of muscular armor—the expression of personality in the way the body moves—shaped such innovations as body psychotherapy (or body-oriented psychotherapy); Gestalt therapy, which focused on patients' apperceptions of a chaotic world; Bioenergetic Analysis, postulating the continuity of body and mind; and Primal Therapy, which concentrates on patients' earliest emotional experiences and encourages verbal expression of childhood suffering.

For many years *Character Analysis* served "as an excellent introduction to psychoanalytic technique."[8] Reich's theory of character derived from Freudian ego-psychology. Character was a kind of "armoring," a rigid outer shell that "protected the individual from the hard knocks of reality," yet, at the same time, "limited his ability to experience life, both within and without him."[9] It is the antithesis of the orgasm and develops, quite

[5] Ibid., p. 134.

[6] Reich, *Die Funktion des Orgasmus* (1927), quoted in Robinson, *Freudian Left*, p. 19.

[7] Elizabeth Young-Bruehl, *Anna Freud: A Biography* (New Haven: Yale University Press, 2008), p. 157.

[8] Richard Sterba, *Reminiscences of a Viennese Psychoanalyst* (Detroit: Wayne State University Press, 1982), p. 35: "This book [*Character Analysis*] serves even today as an excellent introduction to psychoanalytic technique. In my opinion, Reich's understanding of and technical approach to resistance prepared the way for Anna Freud's *Ego and the Mechanisms of Defence* (1936)."

[9] Robinson, *Freudian Left*, p. 23.

literally, "at the expense of the orgasm," consuming the psychic energy not discharged in sexual intercourse. As a consequence, establishing orgastic potency, the ultimate goal of therapy, "involved the dissolution of character and the liberation of psychic energy from its characterological prison." Reich considered his technique of character analysis a contribution to the traditional exploration of the unconscious. "[T]he detection and dissolution of the character's resistance" came to absorb his "entire therapeutic energies."[10]

Character-analytic technique, Reich wrote, was "clinically worked out and tested" in the Vienna Psychoanalytic Clinic between "1925 and 1933," after "the individual and social importance of the function of the orgasm had been recognized only a few years earlier."[11] He called attention to the use of character structure as protective armor to keep the individual from discovering his or her own underlying neuroses.

> I have endeavored to demonstrate that neuroses are the results of a home atmosphere that is patriarchal and sexually suppressive: that, moreover, the only *prophylaxis* worthy of serious consideration is one for the practical implementation of which the present social system lacks every prerequisite; that it is only a thorough turnover of social institutions and ideologies, a turnover that will be dependent upon the outcome of the political struggles of our century.[12]

Reich's theory of character and the technique of character analysis placed him "in the vanguard of the psychoanalytic movement during the 1920's."[13]

He believed that psychology and social and political change were inextricable and that "certain average human structures are native to certain social organizations," and, conversely, that "every social organization produces those character structures which it needs to exist." Following on from his Marxist beliefs, Reich claimed that the ruling class "secures its position, with the help of education and the institutions of the family," making "its ideologies the ruling ideologies of all members of society." Psychology and characterology have the important task: "*to put their*

[10] Ibid., pp. 25–26.

[11] Reich, *Character Analysis*, trans. V.R. Carfagno (New York: Farrer, Straus and Giroux, 1945), pp. xix, xv.

[12] Ibid., p. xxi; emphasis original.

[13] Robinson, *Freudian Left*, p. 28.

finger on the ways and mechanism by means of which man's social entity is transformed into psychic structure, and, thereby, to ideology."[14] Research on character structure "is not of clinical interest only." Given that "character structures are acquired in early childhood and remain intact, without undergoing many changes," they are "*the congealed sociological process of a given epoch.*"[15]

Reich furthermore believed that repressed feelings manifested as muscular tension, and that this mental and physical armor could be overcome by direct manipulation and by making the individual aware of the tension. Reich used the "idea of character defenses that individuals evolved in reaction to anxiety"[16] to treat patients whose neuroses had proved resistant to more orthodox psychoanalytical techniques.

In *The Mass Psychology of Fascism (Massenpsychologie des Faschismus*, 1933), Reich extrapolates: "character-analytic experiences have convinced me that there is not a single individual who does not bear the elements of fascist feeling and thinking in his structure."[17] He applies his findings set out in *Character Analysis* to the rise of fascism: "as a rule, we are dealing with three different layers of the biopsychic structure in the evaluation of human reaction" that "are deposits of social development, which function autonomously":

> On the surface layer of his personality the average man is reserved, polite, compassionate, responsible, conscientious. There would be no social tragedy of the human animal if this surface layer of the personality were in direct contact with the deep natural core. This, unfortunately, is not the case. The surface layer of social cooperation is not in contact with the deep biological core of one's selfhood; it is borne by a *second*, and intermediate character layer, which consists exclusively of cruel, sadistic, lascivious, rapacious, and envious impulses. (xi; emphasis original)

He calls the third layer "the biologic core." If society were decent, people would be "honest, industrious, cooperative, loving, and, if motivated, rationally hating." However, this layer, or "a loosening of the character

[14] Reich, *Character Analysis*, pp. xxi–xxii; emphasis added.

[15] Ibid., p. xxvi; emphasis original.

[16] Dagmar Herzog, *Cold War Freud: Psychoanalysis in an Age of Catastrophe* (Cambridge, UK: Cambridge University Press, 2017), p. 29.

[17] Reich, *The Mass Psychology of Fascism* (1933; rpt. New York: Farrar, Straus & Giroux, 1970), pp. xii-xiv. All references in the text are to this edition.

structure," cannot be reached "without first eliminating the nongenuine spuriously social surface" (xi–xii).

Reich employs the concept of "political psychology" (xviii) to address "the sexual politics of Fascism" and "the Church as a sex-political organization."[18] To him, Fascism is not the modern "act of a Hitler or a Mussolini," but rather "*the expression of the irrational structure of mass man*" (xx; emphasis original). It is the outcome of human history: "*Fascism is the result of man's distortion over thousands of years*" (320, emphasis original). Drawing on his medical experience treating men and women of various classes, races, nations, and religious beliefs, Reich refutes the still generally held notion that Fascism is a specific characteristic of certain nationalities, or a political ideology that is imposed on innocent people by means of force or political maneuvers:

> Fascism is only the organized political expression of the structure of the average man's character, a structure that is confined neither to certain races or nations nor to certain parties, but is general and international ... *'Fascism' is the basic emotional attitude of the depressed man of our authoritarian machine civilization and its mechanistic-mystical conception of life. It is the mechanistic-mystical character of modern man that produces fascist parties, and not vice versa.* (xiii; emphasis original)

"Mystical conception of life" refers to religion—"*Prayer had taken the place of sexual gratification*"—as well as to "*race theory*" based on "*biologic mysticism*," or to Aryan and Nazi historiography founded upon racism, chauvinism, and the mythological Community of Blood and Fate of the German people (154, xx; emphasis original). *Blut und Boden* (blood and soil) was the rallying cry of Nazi racial ideology, which grounded patriotism in a toxic mythology of ethnic ties to the homeland (*Heimat*). "Nazi ideology," declared Reich, as expressed in the phrase "unity of blood and soil,"[19] is based on a mystical "fight of the blood" and, as consequence, on "blood poisoning," "the rise and fall of people," or the "battle between racial values" (83–84, 88).

Depressed by early signs of the Soviet retreat from sexual liberalization, Reich published *Die Sexualität im Kulturkampf: Zur sozialistischen Umstrukturierung des Menschen* (Sexuality in the Culture Struggle:

[18] Reich, *The Sexual Revolution: Toward a Self-Regulating Character Structure*, trans. Therese Pol (New York: Farrar, Straus and Giroux, 1974), pp. xxx.

[19] Ibid., p. xxix.

Toward the Socialist Restructuring of Humanity) in 1936. The second section, which comprises almost half the book, is devoted to "the struggle for a 'new life' in the Soviet Union," where, he argued that "over the past years, news of reactionary sexual and cultural developments ... has accumulated, destroying many hopes."[20] Translated as *The Sexual Revolution: Toward a Self-Governing Character Structure* in 1962,[21] this study analyzes the crisis of bourgeois sexual morality, the failure of attempts at sexual reform that preserved the structure of capitalist society, and the rise and fall of the Soviet sexual revolution.

With *The Mass Psychology of Fascism* and *The Sexual Revolution*, Reich gained a reputation as one of the most radical figures in the history of psychiatry. Along with Erich Fromm and Herbert Marcuse, he emphasized the close connection between psychology and Marxism in defining social and political questions, but he was the first to offer a psychological interpretation of Fascism and Nazism; Fromm's *Fear of Freedom* followed in 1942.

The Sexual Revolution draws extensively on *The Mass Psychology of Fascism*. In the later book, Reich insisted that individual neurosis and "pathological" or "irrational mass behavior" can invariably be traced to the same source, namely sexual repression, which he defined as "an unconscious conflict between instinctual drives for erotic gratification" and "the moral pressure which is needed to keep the dammed-up energies under control."[22] Since "sexual energy is the biological energy which, in the psyche, determines the character of human feeling and thinking," its suppression results not only in psychic and somatic disorders but in "the general disturbance of social functioning manifested in most purposeless actions, mysticism, readiness for war." As such, it constitutes "the mass-psychological basis for the fear of authority, the slavishness, the incredible humbleness on the one hand, and the sadistic brutality on the other."[23] Reich turned psychological *kulturkampf* into sexual *kulturkampf*. Carolyn J. Dean attributes Reich's logic to the view that "healthy sexuality leads to democracy and perverted sexuality leads to fascism."[24]

[20] Ibid., p. 157.

[21] Trans. Theodore P. Wolfe (New York: Macmillan, 1962).

[22] Bennett, *Currency of Desire*, p. 170.

[23] Reich, *The Sexual Revolution: Toward a Self-Regulating Character Structure*, trans. Therese Pol (New York: Farrar, Straus and Giroux, 1974), pp. xxiii, xxv.

[24] Carolyn J. Dean, *Sexuality and Modern Western Culture* (Boston: Twayne Publishers, 1996), quoted by Bennett, *Currency of Desire*, p. 170.

Reich's writings influenced generations of intellectuals. While he himself did not coin the phrase "sexual revolution," according to one historian he acted as its midwife.[25] He left his mark on the sexual revolutions of the so-called Roaring Twenties and the 1960s. His thinking colored Herbert Marcuse's *Eros and Civilization* (1955),[26] and during the 1968 uprisings in Paris and Berlin students scrawled his name on walls and threw copies of *The Mass Psychology of Fascism* at police.[27] Later in life, Reich became a highly controversial figure. His message of sexual liberation perturbed the psychoanalytic community and violated the central taboos of psychoanalysis.

In *The Mass Psychology of Fascism*, Reich was the first to use psychological tools and conceptual frameworks to explain the rise and triumph of modern totalitarian movements. It was followed by Fromm's *Escape from Freedom* (1942); Siegfried Kracauer's *From Caligari to Hitler: A Psychological History of the German Film* (1947), and Erich Neumann's *Depth Psychology and a New Ethic* (1949), with which it has much in common. Like Neumann, Reich looked into the "monster in man" (xii), or in Neumann's rendering, "the shadow", the Jungian archetype of the "dark side," the animal side, of the human soul. "The shadow side of the human race," wrote Neumann, "towers over us all, darkening the sky with its death-rays and its atom bombers."[28]

More generally, Reich's study is the first attempt to explore the psychology of Nazism as an integral part of "the social catastrophes of the twentieth century" (xii). Reich, Fromm, Neumann, and Kracauer all strove to address the same tremendous, acute, and pressing existential problem. Nazism and Fascism ruined their lives and destroyed any illusions they may have had about civilization and progress. They all believed, in Fromm's words, that "If we want to fight Fascism we must understand

[25] James E. Strick, *Wilhelm Reich, Biologist* (Cambridge, MA: Harvard University Press, 2015), p. 2. Wilhelm Heinrich coined the term in *Die Sexual-Revolution* (1921). See Bennett, *Currency of Desire*, p. 168.

[26] Bennett, *Currency of Desire*, p. 169.

[27] David Elkin, "Wilhelm Reich – The Psychoanalyst as Revolutionary," *New York Times*, 18 April 1971, pp. 13–14; Strick, *Wilhelm Reich, Biologist*, p. 2. See also: https://www.nytimes.com/1971/04/18/archives/wilhelm-reich-the-psychoanalyst-as-revolutionary-wilhelm-reich.html

[28] Neumann, *Depth Psychology and a New Ethic* (1949; rpt. London: Hodder and Stoughton, 1969), pp. 19–20.

it."[29] However, Reich was the only one who related Fascism to sexual repression: "'*fascism' is the basic emotional attitude of the suppressed man of our totalitarian machine civilization and its mechanistic-mystical conception of life.*" This modern automaton, programmed with ethnic and religious conceits, frustrations, and resentments, "*produced fascist parties, and not vice versa*" (xiii; emphasis added). His thesis has a close affinity with Horkheimer and Adorno's *Dialectic of Enlightenment*, which sought to reveal why humanity was sinking into "a new kind of barbarism" and to demonstrate a cultural progress that had turned "into its opposite."[30]

Reich's writings reveal a persistent fascination with the paths by which ideologies enter the human psyche. For him, the swastika showed in spectacular fashion how Nazism systematically manipulated the collective unconscious. If for Hitler, "the *swastika*" reflects "the mission of the struggle of the Aryan man," for Reich, it suggests "two interlocked figures" and "acts as a powerful stimulus on deep layers of the organism, a stimulus that proves to be that much more powerful, the more dissatisfied, the more burning with sexual desire, a person is" (102–3). He sees in it the primal scene; in Freudian theory, the moment when children first become aware of their parents' sexual intercourse is deemed crucial in determining their predisposition to future neuroses. In the context of a repressive family, religion, and educational system, political terror, economic exploitation, and sanctioned violence against feared minorities, according to Reich, the individual is absorbed into a poisonous collective unconscious. Nazi political ideology and practice exploited and exacerbated these tendencies to the utmost.

Thus, fighting Fascism required one to study it scientifically using the methods of psychoanalysis. Reich believed that reason alone could check the forces of irrationality and loosen the grip of mysticism; "*natural sexuality is the arch enemy of mystical religion*"; "*sexual consciousness is the end of mysticism*" (178–79; emphasis original); "[*s*]*exual consciousness and mystical sentiments cannot coexist*" (183; emphasis original). Reason, building on a deep respect for life and promoting the harmonious channeling of libido, can inculcate original modes of political action and persuasion. His solution to totalitarianism was "work democracy," a self-managing form

[29] Fromm, *Escape from Freedom* (New York: Rinehart & Company, 1941), p. 5.

[30] Max Horkheimer and Theodor W. Adorno, *Dialectic of Enlightenment: Philosophical Fragments,* ed. Gunzelin Schmid Noerr; trans. Edmund Jephcot (1944; Stanford: Stanford University Press, 2002), pp. xiv, xiii.

of social organization, "developed organically" and regulated "by the function of love, work and knowledge" (xxxi). It would preserve individual freedom and independence and encourage responsibility, based on these principles: "Love, Work and Knowledge are the well-springs of our lives. They should also govern it."[31] Reich boldly contended that "*to define freedom is to define sexual health*" (346; emphasis added).

In more practical terms, *The Mass Psychology of Fascism* argues that the authoritarian family is the first cell and main locus of Fascist society:

> From the standpoint of social development, the family cannot be considered the basis of the authoritarian state, only as one of the most important institutions which support it. We, however, have to look upon it as *political reaction's germ cell*, the most important center for the reproduction of the reactionary men and women. Originating and developing from definite social processes, it becomes the most essential institution for the preservation of the authoritarian system that shapes it. (104–5; emphasis original)

For Reich, the individual's fate and that of entire nations was determined within the confines of the family; through the process of child rearing, the family shapes the character structure that supports the political and economic order of society as a whole. Psychology, politics, and economics are inseparable; economic realities are translated into politics, ethics, and religion.

The French philosopher Gilles Deleuze and psychoanalyst Félix Guattari notably employed Reich's arguments in their joint work *Anti-Oedipus: Capitalism and Schizophrenia* (1972), in which they discuss the formation of fascism at the molecular level of society.[32] They applauded Reich for retrieving Spinoza's important observation in *A Theologico-Political Treatise* (*Tractatus Theologico-Politicus,* 1670): "Why do men fight *for* their servitude as stubbornly as though it was their salvation?"[33] In similar vein, Deleuze and Guattari ask: "after centuries of exploitations, why do people still tolerate being humiliated and enslaved, to such a point, indeed

[31] Reich chose this motto for all his books. It appears in the preamble of *Charakteranalyse* (1933; rpt. 1971); this English translation was used at least as early as *Character Analysis* (1945) and in *The Function of the Orgasm* (1948), a translation of *Die Funktion des Orgasmus* (1927).

[32] Deleuze and Guattari, *Anti-Oedipus: Capitalism and Schizophrenia* (1972; rpt. London: Continuum, 2004), pp. xiii, xviii.

[33] Spinoza, cited in Herzog, *Cold War Freud*, p. 160; emphasis original.

that they *actually want humiliation* and slavery not only for others but for themselves?" They argue that:

> Reich is at his profoundest as a thinker when he refuses to accept ignorance or illusion on the part of the masses as an explanation of fascism, and demands an explanation that will take their desires into account, an explanation formulated in terms of desire: no, the masses were not innocent dupes; under a certain set of conditions, they *wanted* fascism, and it is this perversion of the desire of the masses that needs to be accounted for.[34]

In sum, given that for Reich, "desire produces reality," Deleuze and Guattari argue, he was "the first to raise the problem of the relationship between desire and the social field" and was "the true founder of a materialist psychiatry." By framing the problem in terms of desire, Reich was "the first to reject the explanations of a summary Marxism too quick to say the masses were fooled, mystified."[35] A more recent study stresses that Reich's "early thinking retains a powerful currency in left-wing libidinal economy that figures the sex-drive and the urge to spend as a potentially subversive force to capitalist society."[36]

Reich furthermore made a significant impact on popular culture. In 1971, the Serbian director and screenwriter Dušan Makavejev produced the film *W. R.: Mysteries of the Organism*, which explores the relationship between communist politics and sexuality through the controversial life and work of Austrian-American psychoanalyst Wilhelm Reich. The film's narrative structure is unconventional, intermixing fictional and documentary elements. In 1985, the British singer Kate Bush released *Cloudbusting*, a song about the close relationship between Reich and his young son Peter, told from the perspective of the mature Peter, who describes his memories of their family farm, called Orgonon. There, he and his father spent time trying to produce rain by pointing a machine called a cloudbuster, designed and built by Wilhelm, at the sky. The lyrics go on to relate Wilhelm's abrupt arrest and imprisonment and the young Peter's feelings of pain, loss, and helplessness at being unable to protect his father.[37] The

[34] Deleuze and Guattari, *Anti-Oedipus*, p. 29; emphasis original.

[35] Ibid., pp. 30, 118.

[36] Bennett, *Currency of Desire*, p. 134.

[37] The song ends: "I hid my yo-yo / In the garden / I can't hide you / from the government / Oh, god, daddy / I won't forget / 'Cause every time it rains / You're here in my

song was inspired by Peter Reich's 1973 memoir, *A Book of Dreams*, which Bush read and found deeply moving.

Biographical Sketch

> Wilhelm Reich exchanged his Vienna battlefield for Berlin ... Analysis had lost him before this move, however, because of his unacceptable theoretical technical ideas and because of trouble that his increasing characterological difficulties created in the psychoanalytic community. (Richard F. Sterba, *Reminiscences of a Vienna Psychoanalyst* (p. 82))

Wilhelm Reich (1897–1957), son of Leon Reich and Cecilia (née Roniger) from Galicia, a province in the Austro-Hungarian Empire. He was the elder of two brothers. His father owned a cattle farm in northern Bukovina, another Austrian-Hungarian province. Privately schooled at home up to the age of ten, Reich later attended gymnasium in Czernowitz (Chernivtsi), the capital of Bukovina (today in western Ukraine). However, since Czernowitz was several hundred miles distant from his home, a biographer claims he only went "to the gymnasium once a year to take exams."[38] He excelled at German, Latin, and the natural sciences. Being at Czernowitz broadened his intellectual and cultural horizons and strengthened his Jewish identity, since Jews comprised a third of the city's population. After graduating in 1915, Reich moved to Vienna to stay with his grandmother Roniger, but he was immediately drafted into the Austro-Hungarian army, serving in World War I up until 1918. During the last two years of the war he served as a lieutenant on the Italian front with forty men under his command.

After Reich was discharged in the fall of 1918, he returned to Vienna to begin his academic training. At the turn of the twentieth century the city was restless, full of pioneering artists and exuding abundant intellectual energy. A few years before World War I broke out Vienna's creative milieu experienced a "revelation," almost as if it had foreseen the events to come. Its music, literature, and visual arts broke away from nineteenth-century conservatism. The works of composers Alban Berg, Arnold Schönberg, and Gustav Mahler; writers Stefan Zweig, Arthur Schnitzler, Hugo von

head / Like the sun coming out / Ooh, I..." See, https://genius.com/Kate-bush-cloudbusting-lyrics

[38] Myron Sharaf, *Fury on Earth: A Biography of Wilhelm Reich* (New York: St. Martin's Press, 1983), p. 40.

Hofmannstahl, Rainer Maria Rilke, Georg Trakl, and Karl Kraus; and the unique triad of Gustav Klimt, Egon Schiele, and Oskar Kokoschka in the visual arts define modernism to the present day.

Vienna's cultural contributions are also evident in the philosophy of Ludwig Wittgenstein and the advent of psychoanalysis with Sigmund Freud. Society was turning its gaze inward, away from the monarchy. In 1913, for example, Freud, Adolf Hitler, Leon Trotsky, Joseph Tito, and Joseph Stalin were all living within a few miles of one another in central Vienna, the "city of dreams." Some were regulars at the same coffee-houses. Politics and culture were closely connected as Carl E. Schorske's seminal work *Fin-de-siècle Vienna: Politics and Culture* (1979), describes so well. According to cultural historian J. Sydney Jones: "Gathered in that city were more of the artists and intellectual luminaries who created the modern sensibility than in any other one metropolis."[39] The twenty-year-old Reich returned to this rich and bourgeoning cultural milieu and intellectual atmosphere after the war.

He enrolled at the Faculty of Law at the University of Vienna, but before the end of the semester he switched to the Faculty of Medicine. At the same time, he immersed himself in politics in the "Social Democratic 'youth movement.'"[40] He excelled in his courses, and by his second year he was tutoring first-year students. Apart from his political activity, Reich's most important encounter was with psychoanalysis. He discovered Freud's works in 1919, and soon went to meet the father of psychoanalysis in person. As Reich wrote, Freud "made the strongest and most lasting impression" on him. From that moment, Reich became Freud's "worshipful disciple."[41] While Reich fully acknowledged Freud's "benevolent presence," Freud was very impressed by the student's drive to avoid the "triviality of the everyday."[42] Reich became a rising star in Vienna's psychoanalytic circles, and Freud referred several cases to him in late 1919. With Freud's blessing, Reich began analytical practice in 1920; at the age of 23, he was the youngest instructor in Freud's training institute. After presenting a paper as a guest member of the Vienna Psychoanalytic Society, he was admitted as a regular member.

[39] See http://www.jsydneyjones.com/vienna1900.html

[40] Sharaf, *Fury on Earth*, p. 54.

[41] Ibid., p. 57.

[42] Ibid., p. 58.

Psychoanalysis and politics consumed Reich's energy at that time: "If Reich found in Freud the model par excellence of intellectual daring, he found in the [Social Democratic] youth movement support for his own emotional and social adventurousness."[43] After graduating with a degree in medicine from the University of Vienna in 1922, he became deputy director of Freud's outpatient clinic. In the same year, he helped found the Vienna Seminar for Psychoanalytic Therapy and headed it from 1924 to 1930. A branch of the Vienna Psychoanalytic Society, the seminar was devoted to the improvement of therapeutic technique "through systematic ... studies"[44] of cases that had successfully resisted traditional analysis. As head of this seminar, "Reich established his reputation as a brilliant therapist."[45] He developed important components of his own psychological system—the theory of the orgasm, the theory of character, and the technique of character analysis. "The orgasm was his *ideé fix*. It stood at the heart of his man and society, and *it ultimately became the rubric under which he interpreted the entire cosmos*."[46] As he wrote in his diary on March 1, 1919: "I have become convinced that sexuality is the center around which revolves the whole of social life as well as the inner life of the individual."[47]

Reich was a large man with a cantankerous manner, who managed to look scruffy and elegant at the same time. He sought to reconcile psychoanalysis with Marxism, arguing that neurosis is rooted in sexual and socioeconomic conditions. During his work at the clinic, he visited patients in their homes to observe how they lived and took to the streets with a mobile clinic, promoting adolescent sexuality and the availability of contraceptives, abortion, and divorce, a patently provocative message in Catholic Austria. In 1923, he married Annie Pink. They had two daughters, Eva and Lore. Annie, too, became a practicing analyst.

Over time, however, Reich's relationship with the psychoanalytic community in Vienna deteriorated, and he moved his practice to Berlin in 1930. Richard F. Sterba, who attended the Vienna Psychoanalytic Society's meetings during the early 1920s, provides a firsthand account of Reich's poor scholarship and troubled personality. When Reich presented papers

[43] Sharaf, *Fury on Earth*, pp. 61–2.
[44] Reich, *Function of the Orgasm*, p. 40.
[45] Robinson, *Freudian Left*, p. 13.
[46] Ibid., p. 13; emphasis added.
[47] Reich, quoted in Robinson, *Freudian Left*, p. 13.

on The Perfect Orgasm and the Psychic Disturbances of Orgasm in 1925 and 1926, later included in *The Function of Orgasm*, he revealed "his tendency to reduce the genesis of neurotic symptomology to a monocausal factor." In the ensuing discussions, he increasingly "stubbornly refused to accept any argument that contradicted his theory."[48] He was "the most vociferous defendant of the theory that aggression was caused solely by frustration"[49] and regarded "scientific counterarguments as if they were personal attacks." Accordingly, he "disturbed the scientific calm of the meetings." On such occasions, "he became extremely pale and his facial expression betrayed that he was hardly able to control his rage." As a result, he exchanged "his Vienna battlefield for Berlin in the early 1930s."[50]

The source of Reich's "painfully disrupted human relationships," according to his biographer, can be found in his trauma at losing "both his mother and father"; his mother committed suicide in 1910, and his father intentionally contracted pneumonia and died in 1914. The title of Sharaf's biography, *Fury on Earth*, is most revealing. It fully records Reich's tedious struggles and confrontations throughout his life. The trauma of losing both parents "brought vulnerability – a tendency to repeat his childhood crises in one or another form." Reich's mind was constantly preoccupied by "a question of whom to blame when he and another person or he and another organization quarreled and parted ways."[51]

Reich's unacceptable theoretical and technical ideas as well as his increasing characterological and personal difficulties jeopardized his relationship with Vienna's psychoanalytical community. He became rigid in his technical approach, inhibiting the flexibility and open-mindedness so crucial to analysis. Most troubling, "Reich became more and more sadistic in 'hammering' at the patient's resistive armor." This behavior alienated members and trainers in the seminars, making Reich "embittered and belligerent." Even "Freud could not tolerate Reich's stubborn insistance [sic] on his being right." With dogmatic "fanaticism" Reich maintained that "a perfect orgasm will prevent or cure any form of neurosis." No wonder that younger analysts at these meetings mocked him and his "genital paradise." In Sterba's interpretation, Reich defended this thesis so vigorously because "his character corresponded very much to the 'genital narcissist' he so well

[48] Sterba, *Reminiscences of a Viennese Psychoanalyst*, p. 68.
[49] Ibid., p. 76.
[50] Ibid., p. 82.
[51] Sharaf, *Fury on Earth*, pp. 48–49.

described in one of his papers."[52] Before he moved to Berlin in 1930, Reich's "pathological character traits had become obvious to all." Friends tried to persuade him to undergo a therapeutic analysis to no avail. His ideas "developed more and more into delusions like his orgone theory"—his belief in an esoteric energy or universal life force– "and psychoanalysis lost him for good."[53]

In the political realm, Reich joined the Social Democratic Party of Austria (SPÖ) in 1928 and founded the Socialist Society for Sexual Consultation and Social Research, which advocated "the genital rights of children and adolescents."[54] He joined the Communist Party of Germany (KPD) in November 1930 after moving his psychoanalytic practice to Berlin. Under the KPD umbrella, "Reich's Sex-Pol movement gained some 30.000 supporters among German workers and youth," as it sought to bring about changes to the law and to provide "sex-education … contraception and abortion that would make 'orgastic potency' available to all." Because of his activism on behalf of "the orgasmic rights of children, adolescents and workers," Reich was expelled from the Austrian, German, and Danish Communist parties.[55]

The Sexual Struggle of Youth (*Der Sexuelle Kampf der Jugend*) appeared in 1932 and was followed a year later by what some consider his masterpiece, *Character Analysis* (*Charakteranalyse*), which sought to move psychoanalysis toward a reconfiguration of character structure. Reich argued that character structures were formed to resist facing neuroses. Different character structures, whether schizoid, oral, psychopathic, masochistic, hysterical, compulsive, narcissistic, or rigid, were sustained biologically-physiologically as body types by unconscious muscular contractions. They were the result of social processes; in particular, they reflected the castration and Oedipal anxieties playing out within the nuclear family. Reich submitted this study to the Psychoanalytic Press in Vienna, presided over by Freud who initially accepted it, but then, seeking to distance himself from Reich's politics, cancelled the contract. Reich borrowed money and published the book privately in Vienna.

In 1933, shortly after the Nazis took power, Reich and his family returned to Vienna. His marriage had ended after he began a serious

[52] Sterba, *Reminiscences of a Viennese Psychoanalyst*, p. 87.
[53] Ibid., p. 88.
[54] Reich, *Sexual Revolution*, p. xi.
[55] Bennett, *Currency of Desire*, p. 134.

relationship in May 1932 with Elsa Lindenberg, a dancer with the Berlin State Opera, who was a member of his communist cell. When Reich received an invitation from Danish psychoanalysts and trainers, he left an emotionally and professionally cold Vienna for Denmark on May 1, 1933, and Elsa joined him there.

In August, *The Mass Psychology of Fascism* was privately published in Copenhagen. It defined Soviet Bolshevism as red Fascism, just as vicious as other Fascist forms, particularly German Nazism. No wonder the KPD considered Reich a liability and kicked him out of the party. Reich was expelled from the Danish Communist Party that same year. He was deeply hurt. His exclusion spelled the end of his formal affiliation with the political left, which he had maintained since joining the youth movement in Vienna after World War I.[56] He wrote: "The party was like a second home. So it became to everyone who gives up bourgeois security in favor of the battle for a better future. For many it became the only home."[57]

Reich's book was banned by the Nazis "along with all literature on political psychology" (xviii), and publicly burned along with many other books labeled "un-German." In 1956, during the McCarthy era, the US Food and Drug Administration requested that all of Reich's published works, among them *The Mass Psychology of Fascism*, be burned.

Reich moved from Denmark to Sweden to Norway, where he lived from 1934 to 1939. Owing to his political militancy and social/sexual philosophy, he was expelled from the International Psychoanalytical Association (IPA) in 1934[58] at the Lucerne Congress. He had already been expelled from the German Psychoanalytic Society. He was told that the publication of *The Mass Psychology of Fascism* had made him "a liability to the psychoanalytic movement."[59] This break with the psychology establishment was inevitable. Thus ended the most interesting phase of his career; namely, the period in which he strove to synthesize the ideas of Marx and Freud. Nonetheless, he was right to observe that both Marx and Freud interpreted reality in terms of conflict, be it the class struggle or the conflict among our instincts.

[56] Sharaf, *Fury on Earth*, p. 173.

[57] Reich, *People in Trouble* (1953), quoted in Greenfield, *Wilhelm Reich vs. the USA*, p. 31.

[58] The British psychoanalyst Ernest Jones was probably the chief architect of Reich's expulsion; and, while she later regretted having done so, Anna Freud did not support him.

[59] Robinson, *Freudian Left*, p. 38.

In view of these developments, Reich devoted himself ever more to orgonomy, attempting to measure "orgones," or units of cosmic energy that he believed powered the nervous system. Through his study of human behavior, particularly the libido—instinctual physiological or psychic energy associated with sexual urges—Reich came to believe in the existence of a life force, "orgone energy," produced by "bions," which were microscopic orgone units or energy vesicles in a state of transition between the nonliving and the living. He conceived of mental illness as an orgone deficiency and attempted to treat it by placing the patient in a specially constructed cabinet called an Orgone Energy Accumulator, or orgone box, which he claimed captured and preserved orgone energy in the atmosphere. He subsequently leased orgone boxes as a therapy for various illnesses, including cancer. Following the publication of his research, Reich was accused of scientific charlatanism and in 1939 was forced to flee Norway.

On August 19, he sailed out of Norway on the last ship to leave for the United States before the war broke out on September 3. He accepted an invitation from the New School for Social Research in New York City to serve as an associate professor of medical psychology but lost the position in May 1941 after claiming in a letter to the director that he had saved several lives in secret experiments. In 1942, he purchased an old farm on Dodge Pond in Maine. He started spending summers there and, in 1950, decided to live there year-round.

Reich's experiments, which involved the use of orgone radiation on human subjects, and the commercialization of the orgone box brought him into conflict with the psychological community and the US Food and Drug Administration. In 1947, articles published in *Harper's* and *The New Republic* accused Reich of attributing both neuroses and cancer to unsatisfactory sexual activity.[60] The Federal Trade Commission began to investigate his psychological experiments and concluded that they were completely fraudulent. An investigation into his research was launched, and in 1956 he was charged with criminal contempt of court for violating a 1954 injunction to stop interstate shipment of his publications and equipment, which were burned and destroyed, some by Reich, his friends, and his son Peter.

[60] Greenfield, *Wilhelm Reich vs. the USA*, deals with Reich's ten-year-long legal process, 1947–1957, from the first FDA investigation up until his death in prison in 1957.

The injunction hastened the deterioration in Reich's mental health. From at least early 1954, he came to believe that the planet was under attack by UFOs, or "energy alphas," as he called them. Eventually, he was sentenced to two years in a federal prison, where he died of heart failure in 1957. In retrospect, "some considered this wholesale destruction of Reich's works to be one of the most blatant examples of censorship in U.S. history."[61]

The Mass Psychology of Fascism: Content and Form

> *The Mass Psychology of Fascism* was thought out during the German crisis of 1930–33. (Reich, *The Mass Psychology of Fascism* (p. xvii))

> My book *The Mass Psychology of Fascism* dealt with the sexual politics of Fascism and with the Church as a sex-political organization. (Reich, *The Sexual Revolution* (p. xxx))

> Fascism is only the organized political expression of the structure of the average man's character, a structure that is confined neither to certain races or nations nor to certain parties, but is general and international. (Reich, *The Mass Psychology of Fascism* (p. xiii))

The question at the heart of *The Mass Psychology of Fascism* is why the masses in Germany turned to authoritarianism even though it was clearly against their interests. Reich strove to explain "the social catastrophes of the twentieth century," which, he claimed, resulted from "*the mentality of the 'little man,' who is enslaved and craves authority* and is at the same time rebellious" (xii, xv; emphasis added). Reich was not alone, of course; eight years later, another exile from Nazi Germany, Erich Fromm, turned to this acute, pressing question in his *Escape from Freedom* (1941), asking why "millions in Germany were as eager to surrender their freedom as their fathers were to fight for it; that instead of wanting freedom, *they sought for ways of escape from it*; that other millions were indifferent and did not believe the defense of freedom to be worth fighting and dying for."[62] The trauma of exilic displacement from all they had known and loved drove many to work feverishly toward an answer.

[61] "Wilhelm Reich," *Encyclopædia Britannica*, 2015; Sharaf, *Fury on Earth*, pp. 460–61.
[62] Fromm, *Escape from Freedom*, p. 5; emphasis added.

Reich analyzed the economic and ideological structure of German society between 1928 and 1933. While he dismissed Bolshevism as "red fascism," Germany had chosen Nazism over Communism, he argued, because of its greater propensity toward sexual repression compared to the somewhat more liberal early Bolshevik experiments with sexual revolution. On a lecture tour in Russia in 1929, Reich was very impressed by "progressive institutions such as the State Psychoanalytic Orphanage-Laboratory, in which children of Party members" were raised "without guilt-inducing judgements of punishment for sexual behaviors … obviating all sexual drive problems in their later lives."[63] However, in *The Mass Psychology of Fascism*, he expressed disillusionment: "The removal of individual capitalists and the establishment of state capitalism in Russia in place of private capitalism, ***did not effect the slightest change in the typical helpless, subservient character-structure of masses of people***" (xxvi; emphasis original).

In Germany, Reich believed, the situation was desperate. Children of the proletariat learned from their parents to suppress almost all sexual desire and expended their repressed energy in authoritarian idealism. As adults, any rebellious and sexual impulses they experienced would cause a fundamental anxiety; hence they accepted social control to reduce that anxiety. The fear of revolt as well as of sexuality, he believed, was rooted in the character structure of the German masses, allowing irrational populism to flourish.[64]

> Suppression of the natural sexuality in the child, particularly of its genital sexuality, makes the child apprehensive, shy, obedient, afraid of authority, good and adjusted in the authoritarian sense; it paralyzes the rebellious forces because any rebellion is laden with anxiety; it produces, by inhibiting sexual curiosity and sexual thinking in the child, a general inhibition of thinking and of critical faculties. In brief, the goal of sexual suppression is that of producing an individual who is adjusted to the authoritarian order and who will submit to it in spite of all misery and degradation. Initially, the

[63] Bennett, *Currency of Desire*, pp. 168–69. According to Bennett, Reich "believed communism would make available to all by abolishing the institute of private property that enabled the patriarchal elite to monopolise libidinal spending-power, denying it to others" (pp. 133–34).

[64] On Fascism and sexuality, see the enduringly valuable study by George L. Mosse, *Nationalism and Sexuality: Respectability and Abnormal Sexuality in Modern Europe* (New York: Howard Fertig, 1985), especially ch. 8, "Fascism and Sexuality," pp. 153–80.

> child has to submit to the structure of the authoritarian miniature state, the family, which process makes it capable of later subordination to the general authoritarian system. The formation of the authoritarian structure takes place through the anchoring of sexual inhibition and anxiety.[65]

Elsewhere in his study Reich argues that "[*s*]*exual inhibition prevents the average adolescent from thinking and feeling in a rational way*" (125, emphasis original).

Reich thus inaugurated psychological inquiry into the nature, source, and form of Nazism, and other exiled Jewish intellectuals followed in his path. Like Reich, Fromm and Kracauer leveraged insights from both psychology and Marxism in interpreting Nazi social and political phenomena. Again following Reich, they identified the attractions of Nazism for the German lower middle class.

However, Reich's psychological interpretation of Nazism differed radically from that offered by other exiles from Nazi Germany, who strove to provide social, philosophical, cultural, and political explanations of the trauma of their times. In *Dialectic of Enlightenment* (1944), Horkheimer and Adorno cite the failure of the Enlightenment to explain why humanity was sinking into "a new kind of barbarism" and how cultural progress was turning "into its opposite."[66] Thomas Mann's *Doctor Faustus* (1947) renders Nazi Germany as the new incarnation of the old German legend of amoral arrogance and ambition, equating Germany's covenant with Nazism with a contract with the devil and predicting the same apocalyptic destruction. In *The Myth of the State* (1946), Ernst Cassirer denounces the Aryan racist mythos of *Blut und Boden* (blood and soil), and in *Mimesis: The Representation of Reality in Western Literature* (1946), Erich Auerbach denounces Nazi historiography and Aryan philology, which rejected the Old Testament and Jewish influence on European humanist civilization, history, and culture. He takes up the ancient Greek debate about the respective value of art that imitates or reproduces reality to elevate *mimesis* above myth and ordinary human dignity above specious superheroes. As Hannah Arendt wrote: "All historiography is necessarily salvation and frequently justification."[67] Politics in Nazi Germany determined, to a large

[65] Reich. quoted in Sharaf, *Fury on Earth*, p. 164.

[66] Horkheimer and Adorno, *Dialectic of Enlightenment*, pp. xiv, viii.

[67] Arendt, "A Reply to Erich Vogelin" (1953), in *The Portable Hannah Arendt* (New York: Penguin, 2000), p. 158.

extent, the content and form of all these works that together constitute a grand, multidimensional *Kulturkampf* against Fascism and Nazism.

Contrary to contemporary prevailing views, Reich regarded Fascism, the basic emotional attitude of the suppressed man, as "only the organized political expression of the structure of the average man's character, a structure that is confined neither to certain races or nations nor to certain parties, but is general and international" (xiii). His goal in *The Mass Psychology of Fascism* was to bring about change: "the practical problem of mass psychology is to actuate the passive majority of the population, which always helps political reaction to achieve victory, and to eliminate those inhibitions that run counter to the development of the will to freedom born of the socio-economic situation" (32). In short, Reich develops a plea for rationality in the midst of the tremendous irrational convulsions of the age.

The Mass Psychology of Fascism is a work of synthesis. Reich's idea of "[s]ex-economy was born from the effort that harmonized Freud's depth psychology with Marx's economic theory" (xxiii). By sex-economy he means the manner in which "an individual handles his biological energy; how much of it he dams up and how much of it he discharges orgastically" (xxx). Explaining social and political behavior in these terms "dissolves the contradiction that caused psychoanalysis to forget the social factor and Marxism to forget the animal origin of man." His synthesis of Marx and Freud's theories leads to a new creation: "Psychoanalysis is the mother; sociology is the father of sex-economy. *But a child is more than the sum total of his parents.* He is a new, independent living creature; he is the seed of the future" (xxiii; emphasis original).[68] The merit of Reich's new concept, "sex-economy psychology," lies in adding to the Marxist "economic view of society a new interpretation of man's character and biology." Above all, it provides a new, revolutionary interpretation of psychological history, and a new vision of human nature and the human existential condition in general. This new understanding releases human character from the narrow concepts of bourgeois, capitalist economy; "the human structure with which sex-economic sociology is concerned did not evolve during the past two hundred years," or with the rise of capitalist economy and bourgeois society. On the contrary, it "reflects a patriarchal authoritarian civilization that goes back thousands of years" (xxvi). Again, like Horkheimer and Adorno's *Dialectic of Enlightenment*, Cassirer's *The Myth*

[68] From 1929 to 1935 Reich wrote six books in which he sought to provide an intellectual reconciliation between Marx and Freud. See Robinson, *Freudian Left*, p. 40.

of the State, and Auerbach's *Mimesis*, in which the analysis commences with the Old Testament or the Greeks, Reich offers a deep, historical, psychological understanding of human history spanning thousands of years. For them all, each in his own discipline, the contemporary problem, Fascism and Nazism, called for a thorough deconstruction of Western culture and civilization.

Reich offered a new, overarching historical and psychological interpretation: "Twentieth-century fascism ... raised the basic question of *man's character, human mysticism and craving for authority*, which covered a *period of some four to six thousand years*" (xxvi; emphasis original). The causes of "the abominable excesses of the capitalist era," such as predatory imperialism and racial subjugation, are not new but rather a direct continuation of "the human structure of the untold masses who had endured all this" and "had become totally dependent upon authority, incapable of freedom." This age-old subjugation, rather than Marxist class struggle, is the essential power that drives and shapes history. Reich acknowledges that "the point of view of sex-economic biophysics is, in the strict and positive sense of the word, infinitely more radical than that of the vulgar Marxists" (xxvi-xxvii; emphasis original).

In practical terms, "the social measures of the past three hundred years can no longer cope with the mass pestilence of fascism." Therefore, he offers an alternative: "*the discovery of natural biological work-democracy in international human intercourse is to be considered the answer to fascism*" (xxvii; emphasis original). Work-democracy will mean that "for the first time in the history of sociology, a *possible* future regulation of human society is derived not from ideologies or conditions that must be created, but from natural processes that have been present and have been developing from the very beginning" (xxxi; emphasis original). It "*is borne by the functions of love, work and knowledge and is developed organically. It fights mysticism and the idea of the totalitarian state not through political attitudes but through practical functions of life, which obey their own laws*" (xxxi; emphasis added).

Psychology, history, and Fascism are interwoven and inseparable in Reich's system; psychology, or the psychological understanding of the course and progress of history, exposes the poverty of Fascism and Nazism by providing a meaningful and fruitful alternative. Society should be based on natural, sexual drives, not invented, oppressive ideological conditions. In light of these contentions, we see why during the 1968 uprisings in Paris and Berlin, enthusiastic students scrawled Reich's name on walls and threw copies of *The Mass Psychology of Fascism* at police. His work-democracy is a radical alternative not only to Fascism and Nazism, but also to capitalism as a whole.

Mass Psychology: Sexual Suppression and Repression

> Fascist mysticism is orgastic yearning, restricted by mystic distortion and inhibition of natural sexuality. (Reich, *The Mass Psychology of Fascism* (p. xxi))

As a communist living in Germany from 1930 to 1933, Reich was well aware of the Marxists' failure to comprehend the rise and triumph of Nazism. "The Marxists," he wrote in *The Mass Psychology of Fascism*, "*had failed to take into account the character structure of the masses and the social effect of mysticism*" (5; emphasis original). He meant here *völkisch* mysticism, an outgrowth of nineteenth-century romanticism that conceived the German people as one in a toxic mythology of blood and homeland (*Heimat*). In sexual terms, "*fascist mysticism is orgastic yearning, restricted by mystic distortion and inhibition of natural sexuality*" (xxi; emphasis original). Marx and Engels, wrote Reich, "were not familiar" with "the *new* historical realities." "Vulgar Marxism" viewed the crisis of 1929–1933 in terms of "chauvinism" and "psychosis," but a keen observer could see that "not only regressive but also very energetic progressive social forces emerged in the rebelliousness of the lower middle class, which later constituted the *mass basis* of fascism" (6; emphasis original). Instead of leading leftward, the German crisis "led to an extreme development to the Right in the ideology of the proletarian strata of population" (7–8). Vulgar Marxists accepted the view that the masses had been betrayed, overlooking the growing "cleavage" between the "economic basis," which motivated the left, and "the ideology of broad layers of society, which developed to the Right." As a result, "a distressed middle class" tended "to become radical Rightist." More specifically, "fascism was directed against the upper middle class and hence could not be disposed of '*merely*' as a bulwark of big finance, if only because it was a mass movement" (8; emphasis original).

Contrary to the implicit "mechanistic materialism" (23) of vulgar Marxists, who focused exclusively on economic considerations, Reich held that to gain an understanding of "the role of ideology and the emotional attitudes of these masses" as "a historical factor" one must investigate their character structure (10). He argued that "*it was not the economic but the ideological distribution that was decisive*" and that "the political importance of the lower middle class is greater than had been assumed" (13; emphasis original). Vulgar Marxist interpretations totally failed to grasp "the nature of the psychological structure of the masses and its relation to the economic basis from which it derives" (14). They brushed aside "psychology, which is not supposed to be 'Marxistic,'" deeming it "a metaphysical system pure and simple." Hence, they rejected "this 'subjective factor of history'" (14–16).

"Character-analytic psychology," by contrast, filled the gap in narrow economic interpretations "by revealing the process of man's psychic life, which is determined by the conditions of existence." This method "puts its finger on the 'subjective factor,' which the vulgar Marxists had failed to comprehend." Subjective factors, rather than objective economic considerations, validate "political psychology," which emerged as a crucial field of inquiry for those seeking to explain the nature and form of Nazism. When political psychology is "specialized in the investigation of typical psychic processes *common* to one category, class, professional group, etc. and excludes individual differences, then it becomes a *mass psychology*," the title and marrow of Reich's book (16; emphasis original).

By definition, mass psychology deals with "the most private and most personal and highest accomplishments of human instinct and thought," or, in other words, with "*the sexual life of women and adolescents and children, the level of the sociological investigation of these conditions and its application to new social questions*." Against this psychological and sociological background, which constituted the essence of the "human condition," argued Reich, "Hitler was able to bring about a historical situation that is not to be ridiculed out of existence." Marx could not develop "a sociology of sex, because at that time sexology did not exist." Now, the picture had radically changed: "ideology becomes a material force" with "the ability to arouse the masses" to form a "Hitler psychosis" (17; emphasis original).[69] Only psychology could explain how ideology became a material force. Reich argued that when ideology – that is, a set or system of ideas about nation, race, or religion that can incite people to action –

[69] For psychological interpretations of Hitler's charisma, see Ron Rosenbaum, *Explaining Hitler: The Search for the Origins of His Evil* (New York: De Capo Press, 2014); Robert G. L. Waite, *The Psychological God: Adolf Hitler* (New York: Basic Books, 1977); Rudolph Binion, *Hitler among the Germans* (New York: Elsevier, 1976); and Bertram Henry Schaffner, *Father Land: A Study of Authoritarianism in the German Family* (New York: Columbia University Press, 1948).

has a "repercussive effect upon the economic process ... it must have become a material force" (18).

Understanding the masses' emotional response to ideology as a historical factor led Reich to embed "the economic process in the *psychic structure of the people who make up the society.*" He noted a contradiction between "the influence exercised" by "material position" and by "the ideological structure of society." Since social ideology "*changes man's psychic structure, it has not only reproduced itself in man but, what is more significance, has become an active force, a material power in man*" (18; emphasis original). Modes of belief and persuasion lead to modes of action and conduct. Based on these assumptions, Reich turned to mass psychology as a way to interpret Fascist power.

"Mass psychology" is based on the observation that "the economic and ideological situations of the masses need not necessarily coincide." Indeed, argued Reich, "there can be a considerable cleavage between the two." The "vulgar Marxists," who "do not acknowledge psychology," tended to explain everything in terms of economic conditions, yet ignorance about "the character structure of the masses of people" was leading them nowhere (19–20). Communists and Social Democrats commonly claimed that "fascism had 'befogged,' 'corrupted,' and 'hypnotized' the masses," yet these imputations proved "sterile." Most important, such explanations "do not convince the masses" themselves because "social economic inquiry by itself is not enough." The individual's psychic structure derives from "the social situation" on the one hand and "the entire atmosphere of authoritarian society" on the other (21). The "middle-class man" might "rebel against the 'system,'" yet at the same time, "he fears progress and becomes extremely reactionary." The Marxist "socio-economic point of view," or "mechanistic materialism," could not explain such an overt contradiction; mass psychology could (21–23).

Reich believed that "to explain Hitler's success solely on the basis of National Socialist demagogy, the 'befogging of the masses,' their 'deception,' or to apply the vague, hollow term 'Nazi Psychosis,' as the Communists and other politicians" did, was wrong. Why were the masses "*accessible to deception, befogging, and a psychotic situation*"? Without psychological knowledge of "what *goes on in the masses*, the problem cannot be solved" (35–36; emphasis original). To say that the success of the National Socialist German Workers' Party (NSDAP) "is inconsistent" with the view that the "Hitler movement was a reactionary movement" that led to the suppression of the masses, merely restates the question. Why would "millions upon millions affirm their own suppression" by voting for Hitler and his party? This clear contradiction can be explained only by investigating mass psychology, "not by politics or economics" (36).

Mass psychology is essential to explaining not only the cause and origins of Fascism and Nazism, according to Reich, but also world wars: "we have to ask how the *psychological structure of the masses* was capable of absorbing the imperialist ideology, to translate the imperialist slogans into deeds that were diametrically opposed to the peaceful, politically disinterested attitude of the German population" (22; emphasis original). This phenomenon can be understood "only from the sex-economic point of view"; namely, by grasping that the "*imperialistic ideology concretely changed the structures of the working masses to suit imperialism.*" More specifically and according to Marxist reasoning, "*every social order produces in the masses of its members that structure which it needs to achieve its main aims*" (22–23; emphasis original). Ideology transformed into material force understood that "no war would be possible without this psychological structure of the masses." Psychology explains not only this internal German political and social crisis but also numerous international crises, such as world wars: "the *contradictions* in the economic structure of society are also embedded in the psychological structure of the subjugated masses" (23; emphasis original).

Reich was not afraid to criticize Marx and Lenin for their failure to comprehend the "*irrational, seemingly purposeless actions*" of the masses, which give clear evidence of "*the cleavage between economy and ideology*" (23; emphasis original). The working man, he wrote, is "neither a clear-cut reactionary nor a clear-cut revolutionary" but caught in "a contradiction between reactionary and revolutionary tendencies." The result is "a mode of action that offsets the conservative psychic forces with revolutionary forces" (24).

Reich found the solution to this contradiction in the realm of psychology. He quoted Lenin, reflecting on the irrational behavior of the masses before and during the 1905 soldiers' revolt in Russia; on the one hand, the soldiers had a great deal of sympathy with the cause of the peasant; on the other, they wavered, negotiated with their superior officers, then submitted to the rod. In "their officers the soldiers of 1905 unconsciously perceived their childhood fathers (condensed in the conception of God), who denied sexuality and whom one could neither kill nor want to kill, though they shattered one's joy of life" (32). This explanation may seem naïve and simple, but it represents a serious effort to explain "a contradiction between reactionary and revolutionary tendencies" (24).

While the "vulgar Marxist" simply disregards the Russian soldiers' psychology, the Freudian conception recognizes "such behavior as the effect of infantile guilt-feelings toward the father." However, the Freudian conception also fails to provide "any insight into the sociological origin and function of such behavior" because it "overlooks *the connection between this behavior and the repression and distortion of the sexual life of the broad masses*" (25; emphasis added). *The Mass Psychology of Fascism* launched a criticism of both Marxism and Freudian psychoanalysis. The chapter on "Ideology as a Material Force" expands on the content and form of the concept of *ideology* to encompass psychological drive and inclination.

To clarify the nature of "irrational *mass* psychological phenomena," Reich turned to "*sex-economy*," a term he derived from "the sociology of human sexual life" that deals with "the social function of sexual repression" (24–25; emphasis original). Marx, he contended, "found social life to be governed by the conditions of economic production and by the class conflict that resulted from these conditions at a definite point in history." More often than not, the main weapon of the ruling class is its "ideological powers over the oppressed, for it is this ideology that is the mainstay of the state apparatus." However, the character structure of man, "the so-called 'subjective factor of history' in Marx's sense," remained uninvestigated because the father of historical materialism was "a sociologist and not psychologist." Marx and his followers could not explain why human beings allowed themselves to be exploited and humiliated, why they had submitted to slavery for thousands of years. Marx had ascertained "only the economic process of society and the mechanism of economic exploitation" (25–26).

About half a century after Marx came Freud, who used the method of psychoanalysis to discover "the process that governs psychic life." Freud found, first, that consciousness is only a small part of psychic life, "governed by psychic processes that take place unconsciously" and are not accessible "to conscious control." Eventually, psychoanalysis deteriorated into a kind of "physic of the brain," "brain mythology"; "a mysterious objective *Geist*," or spirit, entered "the domain of natural science."

Freud's second great discovery was that "even the small child developed a lively sexuality, which has nothing to do with procreation." Therefore, "*sexuality and procreation*, and *sexual* and genital, are not the same." Researchers, Reich among them, asserted that "sexuality, or rather its energy, the *libido*" is "the prime motor of psychic life." Thus, "the biological presuppositions and social conditions of life overlap in the mind" (26; emphasis original).

Freud's third great discovery was that childhood sexuality, "of which what is most crucial in the child-parent relationship ('the Oedipus complex') is a part, is usually repressed out of fear of punishment for sexual acts and thoughts (basically a 'fear of castration'); the child's sexual activity is blocked and extinguished from memory." However, unconscious, these sexual desires do not weaken. Repression intensifies them, and they produce "various pathological disturbances of the mind." In view of these discoveries, Freud could claim that "he had all humanity as his patient" (26–27).

Finally, Freud's fourth important discovery is related to human nature; "far from being of divine origin, man's moral code was derived from the educational measures used by the parents and parental surrogates in earlier childhood." Essentially, these educational measures were "most effective" in suppressing childhood sexuality and later sparked a "conflict between instinct and morality *within* the person." The moral code assisted in supporting "sexual repression" (27; emphasis original).

Freud's psychological discoveries clearly contrasted with accepted "moral philosophy," especially "religious metaphysics, both of which uphold eternal moral values, conceive of the world as being under the rulership of an objective 'power,' and deny childhood sexuality." Yet psychology too would fail to enlighten us:

> Psychoanalytic sociology tried to analyze society as it would analyze an individual, set up an absolute antithesis between the process of civilization and sexual gratification, conceived of destructive instincts as primary biological facts governing human destiny immutably, denied the existence of a matriarchal primeval period, and ended in crippling skepticism, because it recoiled from the consequences of its own discoveries. (27)

At this point, Reich allows himself a personal statement: all the shortcomings of psychoanalytic sociology have "not the slightest effect on our determination to defend Freud's great discoveries against every attack, regardless of origin or source" (27–28). To redeem current psychoanalytic sociology, Reich offers "sex-economy sociology". By incorporating the insights afforded by psychoanalysis, he argues, "sociology attains a higher standard and is in a much better position to master reality." It can "finally" comprehend the structure he outlined in *Character Analysis*. The genuine sociologist will appreciate the "comprehension of childhood sexuality as a highly significant revolutionary act" (28). His science of sex-economy sociology, "born from the effort to harmonize Freud's depth psychology with Marx's economic theory," Reich boasts, "*dissolves the contradiction that caused psychoanalysis to forget the social factor and Marxists to forget the animal origin of man*" (xxiii; emphasis added). Sex-economy sociology is built upon "the *sociological* groundwork of Marx and the *psychological* groundwork of Freud [and] is essentially a mass psychological and sex-sociological science at the same time. Having rejected Freud's philosophy of civilization, it begins where the clinical psychological line of questioning of psychoanalysis ends" (28; emphasis original).

While psychoanalysis discloses the mechanisms of sexual suppression and repression and their "pathological consequences in the individual," sex-economic sociology, the field Reich created, asks: "*For what sociological reasons is sexuality suppressed by the society and repressed by the individual?*" (28; emphasis original). The church claimed this was necessary for salvation; philosophers claimed human ethics and morality demanded it, and "Freudian philosophy of civilization" claimed it was "in the interest of 'culture.'" Reich was not convinced. How could "the masturbation of small children and the sexual intercourse of adolescents … disrupt the building of gas stations or the manufacturing of airplanes?" Clearly, sexual suppression and repression were related, not to culture, but rather "to social order." An inquiry into the history of sexual suppression reveals, he argued, that it has no bearing on cultural development, for it "was not until relatively late, with the establishment of an authoritarian patriarchy and the beginning of the division of the classes, that suppression of sexuality begins to make its appearance." With it, "the nature of human feeling changes; a sex-negating religion comes into being and gradually develops its own sex-political organization, the church with all its predecessors, the aim of which is nothing other than the eradication of man's sexual desires and consequently of what little happiness there is on earth" (29). Like Fromm and Neumann, Reich turns from explaining the psychology of Nazism to an overarching psychological interpretation of human civilization.

Faithful to his Marxist reasoning, Reich justifies his new analysis from "the perspective of the now-thriving exploitation of human labor" (29). At the core of Reich's interpretation, sexual suppression and human exploitation are closely connected: "*The interlacing of the socio-economic structure with the sexual structure of society and the structural reproduction of society take place in the first four or five years in the authoritarian family* ... Thus, the authoritarian state gains an enormous interest in the authoritarian family. *It becomes the factory in which the state's structure and ideology are molded*" (30; emphasis original). Reich had found the Archimedean point (*Punctum Archimedis*) at which the sexual and the economic interests of the authoritarian system converge.

The family is the incubator of the authoritarian state; within its boundaries, moral inhibitions were imposed on children's natural sexuality, making them "afraid, shy, fearful of authority, obedient, 'good' and 'docile' in the authoritarian sense of the words." It debilitates "man's rebellious forces," tethering "every vital life-impulse" with "severe fear," and "since sex is a forbidden subject, thought in general and man's critical faculty also become inhibited." The only objective of the imposed morality is to produce "acquiescent subjects" who are "adjusted to the authoritarian order." In sum, the "family is the authoritarian state in miniature." It grafts "*sexual inhibitions and fear in the living substance of sexual impulses*" to bend the most powerful human drives toward order (30; emphasis original). This dark description of the human condition could perhaps have been written only in Germany during the first half of the twentieth century.

In political terms, Reich argued, "sexual repression strengthens political reaction." It makes the "individual in the masses passive and nonpolitical" and transforms human "structure" to support "the authoritarian order." At this point, he develops the idea of psychological projection, a defense mechanism through which the human ego defends itself against unconscious impulses or qualities (both positive and negative) by attributing them to others, but never to itself. Projection incorporates blame shifting; for example, a habitually rude person may constantly accuse others of being rude. "When sexuality is prevented from attaining its natural gratification, owing to the process of social repression ... it seeks various kinds of substitute gratifications." At the extreme, "natural aggression is distorted into brutal sadism." This tendency is enlisted to recruit the masses to fight and die in "imperialistic wars that are instigated by a few" (31). Erich Neumann uses the concept of projection in *Depth Psychology and a New Ethic* (1949), where he argues that for the individual, "evil cannot be acknowledged as 'his own evil' at all" but is seen "as something alien, and the victims of shadow projection are therefore, always and everywhere, the aliens"[70]—Jews, blacks, migrants. Projection obviates personal responsibility, Reich observes, while sexual repression "inhibits the will to freedom." More fundamentally, it "*changes the structure of economically suppressed man in such a way that he acts, feels, and thinks contrary to his own material interest*" (32; emphasis original).

In concluding this chapter on "Ideology as a Material Force," Reich argues that "*the practical problem of mass psychology is to actuate the passive majority of the population*, which always helps political reaction to achieve victory, and to eliminate those inhibitions that run counter to the development of the will to freedom born of the socio-economic situation" (32; emphasis added). These words only confirm the harrowing reality in Germany when Hitler rose to power in 1933, yet Reich's main concern is to offer an authentic alternative. He finds ready examples in football, laughter, and music, where the masses' psychological energy is not restrained: "Freed of its bonds and directed into the channels of the freedom movement's rational goals, *the psychic energy of the average mass of people excited over a football game or laughing over a cheap musical*" could "*no longer be ... fettered*" (33–34; emphasis added).

Reich's vision of a post-repressed society freed of sexual inhibitions influenced the "sexual revolution" of the late 1960s in the West.

The Family's Authoritarian Ideology and Mass Psychology

If, as Reich argued, psychoanalysis is "the mother" and sociology "the father of sex-economy" (xxiii), it follows that he found "*the key to the emotional foundation of the structure*" of authoritarian ideology (48; emphasis original) within the confines of the family. Rather than the economic sphere, the source of fascism can be traced to the family's ties and bonds, emotions, sentiments, and sensations, its content and its form. Above social, political, and economic considerations, it is psychology that holds the key to unlock the mystery of authoritarian appeal; it alone can propound plausible explanations about fascism's nature and power. The tools of psychology are needed to explore the "*emotions* of the individuals in the masses" (34; emphasis original).

[70] Neumann, *Depth Psychology and a New Ethic* (1949, rpt. London, Hodder and Stoughton, 1969), p. 140.

Here lies Reich's unique and significant contribution to demystifying the rise of Fascism and Nazism. In psychological terms, a leader, or *Führer*, "can be successful ... only *if his personal point of view, his ideology, or his program bears resemblance to the average structure of a broad category of individuals.*" Thus, "[*o*]*nly when the structure of the führer's personality is in harmony with the structure of broad groups can a 'führer' make history*" (34–36; emphasis original). Psychology can unveil the masses' emotional attachment to a leader, which explains Nazism and Fascism better than political and economic factors.

In *Escape from Freedom,* Fromm too strove to explain why, after World War I, "new systems emerged which denied everything that men believed they had won in centuries of struggle." Totalitarian movements like Fascism and Nazism "effectively took command of man's entire social and personal life" and effected "the submission of all but a handful of men to an authority over which they had no control."[71] The "vast majority of the population" in Germany, continues Fromm, "was seized with the feeling of individual insignificance and powerlessness," a psychological dynamic that "Nazism resurrected."[72]

Reich, Fromm, and Kracauer all looked to the psychology of the lower middle class because they held it responsible for the rise and triumph of Nazism. According to Reich, "*National Socialism was a lower middle-class movement*" (41; emphasis original). Hitler relied upon "the various strata of the lower middle class for his support." Reich's identification of the lower middle class with Hitler is based on the "psychic process" that begins in "the first years" of raising a child in an "authoritarian family atmosphere." This class especially enforced the "sexual inhibitions and debilitations" that constituted not only "the most important requisites for the existence of the authoritarian family" but "the most essential groundwork of ... the formation of the lower middle-class" (54). By means of projection, people of that lower middle-class saw themselves as belonging to the upper middle class or the elite because of their education.

The cardinal question is "[w]hy *do the masses allow themselves to be politically swindled?*" People had every opportunity to assess the parties' positions but failed "to see that, while promising the workers that the owners of the means of production would be disappropriated, Hitler promised the capitalists that their rights would be protected" (36; emphasis original).

[71] Fromm, *Escape from Freedom*, pp. 4–5; emphasis added.

[72] Ibid., pp. 217, 221.

Reich turned to Hitler's *Mein Kampf* (*My Struggle*, 1925–1926) to consider its reflection of the "authoritarian ideology of the family in the mass psychology of Fascism" (34). Erik H. Erikson (née Salomonsen) did the same in *Childhood and Society* (1950), where he claims:

> For nations, as well as for individuals, are not only defined by their highest point of civilized achievement, but also by the weakest one in their collective identity: they are, in fact, defined by the distance, and the quality of the distance, between these points. National Socialist Germany has provided a clear-cut illustration of the fact that advanced civilization is potentially endangered by its own advance, in that it splits ancient conscience, endangers incomplete identities, and releases destructive forces.[73]

Having devoted their psychological research to childhood, both Reich and Erikson drew conclusions about Germans' attraction to and responsibility for Nazism from Hitler's childhood and youth as described in *Mein Kampf*. To them, Hitler was the embodiment of lower middle-class psychology: Reich observed that "the nationalistic führer is the personification of the nation" (62).

Reich's criticism of Fascist and Nazi sexuality was rather hastily formulated and was based primarily on *Mein Kampf*. Recent studies, however, show that Nazi attitudes toward sexuality were complex and not as rigidly defined or negatively oriented as he would have us believe. For example, in her numerous studies, Dagmar Herzog illuminates the problematic Nazi views of sexuality during the 1930s and thereafter. Reich's sought to wage a *Kulturkampf*, or cultural war, against Nazism and Fascism; hence, he highlighted their negative views and overlooked any variety in their sexual behavior and persuasions. Paradoxically, Reich, who blamed the 'vulgar Marxists' for failing to comprehend the complexity of the spell the Nazis cast on the masses, was rather narrow-minded in his understanding of Nazism and its sexuality. A few examples are in order here.

In her essay "Hubris and Hypocrisy, Incitement and Disavowal: Sexuality and German Fascism," Herzog repudiates the thesis about the "National Socialists' fear of sexuality" and claims that the Third Reich was simply "sex-hostile." The distinctive innovation of Nazi sexual politics was "the attempt to harness popular liberalizing impulses and growing preoccupation with sex to a racist, elitist, and homophobic agenda," and not

[73] Erikson, *Childhood and Society* (London: Imago Publishing, 1950), pp. 284–85.

"so much to suppress sexuality." The Nazi pedagogue Alfred Zeplin announced in 1938 that "*Sexual activity is not sinful, it is sacred.*" Likewise, the journal of the Schutzstaffel (SS; literally protection squadron), *Das Schwarze Korps* (*The Black Corps*), "aligned itself with young people impatient with traditional bourgeois mores." Just as sexually conservative Nazi mores were expressed through anti-Semitism, "so also were Nazis' particular versions of sexually emancipatory ideas." Herzog concludes: "The issue that requires emphasis here is that all the ugly aspects of Nazi sexual politics and other politics were not embedded in a broader antisexual attitude."[74]

Conclusion

> Fascism is the vampire leeches to the body of the living, the impulse to murder given free rein, when love calls fulfilment in spring. (Reich, *The Mass Psychology of Fascism* (p. xvii))

The bad reputation Reich earned through his bizarre experiments, his use of "orgone radiation" on human subjects, and the commercialization of the orgone box, should not deter us from appreciating his unique and important contribution to our understanding of Nazism and Fascism. Well before Erich Fromm, Siegfried Kracauer, and Erik Erikson, he developed a psychological analysis of the mass attraction to totalitarianism, and well before Fromm, Kracauer, and Herbert Marcuse, he emphasized the combined usefulness of psychology and Marxism in explaining social and political events. Reich was the first to point to psychology's crucial role in history. The outcome was *The Mass Psychology of Fascism* (1933), which contains many important insights and is read with great interest to this day.

Reich's main contribution lies in revealing the individual-level psychological structures that lead to support for authoritarian regimes. Today, in the second decade of the twenty-first century, the rise of various reactionary, anti-liberal movements in Europe and the United States, which challenge their countries' stated democratic principles, not to mention those in China, Russia, and nations in southeast Asia, Latin America, and the Muslim world, merely affirms Reich's singular insights regarding the

[74] In *Sexuality and German Fascism*, ed. Dagmar Herzog (New York: Berghahn Books, 2005), pp. 4, 11, 18. See also Herzog, *Cold War Freud: Psychoanalysis in an Age of Catastrophe* (Cambridge, UK: Cambridge University Press, 2017).

"fascist character" (xvi) and the reasons why human beings fight for their own oppression. In the face of simplistic Marxist interpretations, Reich refused to accept that the masses were too ignorant, corrupt, or deluded to oppose the rise of Fascism. Instead, he acknowledged their frustrations and desires and peered deeply into their origins. He raised the torch of psychology as a crucial tool in elucidating social and political change. He argued that "social economic inquiry by itself is not enough", and that the individual's psychic structure derives, on the one hand, from "the social situation" but, on the other, "from the entire atmosphere of authoritarian society" (21). People who "rebel against the 'system'" can also fear change and burrow into convention and radical conservatism (21–23).

This dualism is intrinsic to "the fascist character" (xvi) and explains why the masses acceded to "*deception, befogging, and a psychotic situation.*" Without knowing precisely "what *goes on in the masses,*" we cannot understand their self-destructive behavior (35–36; emphasis original). *The Mass Psychology of Fascism* argues that emotions and desires must be taken into account: "*'Fascism' is the basic emotional attitude of the depressed man of our authoritarian machine civilization and its mechanistic-mystical conception of life*" (xiii; emphasis original). Reich was the prophet of psychological analysis of social and political questions. According to Deleuze and Guattari, he was "the first to raise the problem of the relationship between desire and the social field."[75]

Reich was crucially influenced by the rise of Fascism in Germany and Italy, which led him to abandon "vulgar Marxist" explanations. He wrote his book just as "the mysticism of the National Socialists" that "triumphed over the economic theory of socialism" led to the election of Hitler in 1933 (5). At that time Fascism was generally regarded as a "political party," but Reich contended that this simple ascription failed to take account of "*the character structure of the masses and the social effect of mysticism*" (5; emphasis original). Fascism was the "organized political expression of the structure of the average man's character." It was "an *international* phenomenon, which pervades all the bodies of human society of *all* nations." He drew this conclusion upon considering "the international events of the past fifteen years" (xiii; emphasis original). Psychology exposed the agonies festering in history. It showed that "there is not a single individual who does not bear the elements of fascist feeling and thinking in his structure" (xiii–xiv). Fascism, "in its pure form," was

[75] Deleuze and Guattari, *Anti-Oedipus*, p. 118.

"the sum and total of all the irrational reactions of the average human character" (xiv). Moreover, Reich claimed that "racial theory is not a product of fascism," but rather "fascism ... is a product of racial hatred and is its politically organized expression." Thus, there was "a German, Italian, Spanish, Anglo-Saxon, Jewish and Arabian fascism." He saw race ideology as "*a pure biopathic expression of the character structure of the orgastically impotent man*" (xiv; emphasis original). Again, only psychology could explain Fascism and Nazism and racism.

No one else talked about Fascism and Nazism in this way during the 1930s; no one defined human character structure as a Pandora's Box from which all the horrors of modern history had escaped. Reich's study of the mass psychology of fascism revealed its true nature, including its roots in sexual perversion and sadism: "Fascism countenances that religiosity that stems from *sexual perversion*, and it transforms the masochistic [sic] character of the old patriarchal religion of suffering into *sadistic religion*. In short, *it transposes religion from the 'other-worldliness' of the philosophy of suffering to the 'this worldliness' of sadistic murder* (xv; emphasis added). In simpler terms, the fascist mentality is the mentality of "the little man." He is "the drill sergeant"—as brilliantly portrayed in Stanley Kubrick's film *Full Metal Jacket* (1987) or Edward Zwick's film *Glory* (1989)—"in the colossal army of our deeply sick, highly industrialized civilization." In his extensive and thorough study of the suppressed little man's character, Reich concludes that "an intimate knowledge of his backstage life, are indispensable prerequisites to an understanding of the forces fascism builds upon" (xv).

Again and again, Reich reveals the hidden psychological elements of Fascism through the little man, or the man of the lower middle class, exposing the dark abysses of racism, sadism, and masochism. He believed that Fascism "can be crushed only if it is countered *objectively* and *practically* with well-grounded knowledge of life's processes" (xvi; emphasis original). Erich Fromm agreed when he wrote in 1941: "If we want to fight Fascism, we must understand it."[76] For both, knowledge is power.

In his fight against Fascism and Nazism, Reich did not mince words: "Fascism is the vampire leeches to the body of the living, the impulse to murder given free rein, when love calls fulfilment in spring" (xvii). Through his "political psychology" he sought to discover "the human structure of the untold masses" who had become "totally dependent upon

[76] Fromm, *Escape from Freedom*, p. 5.

authority, incapable of freedom and extremely accessible to mysticism" (xxvii); and to propose an alternative—a way to recover freedom, love, fulfillment, and spring. To Reich's credit, in his times and given his burdens, no one did it better than he.

This is also the reason why Reich continues to inspire us to this day. Clear evidence of this can be found in the moving poem "Cloudbusting" (1985) by the English singer-songwriter and record producer Kate Bush:

> Oh, god, daddy
> I won't forget
> 'Cause every time it rains
> You're here in my head

A Psychological Inquiry into Totalitarianism: Erich Fromm's *Escape from Freedom*

Erich Fromm was a German social psychologist and psychoanalyst who was associated with the Frankfurt School of Critical Theory. He was known for developing the concept that freedom was a fundamental part of human nature and for challenging the theories of Sigmund Freud. In his works he presented the view that understanding of basic human needs is essential to the understanding of society and mankind. In *Escape from Freedom* Fromm explores humanity's shifting relationship with freedom, with particular regard to the personal consequences of its absence.

Fromm's Life and Works

> Fromm helped to pave an alternative path for his day and for ours, one contoured by love and what he called humanism. The goal was to promote a joyous and caring community where the love of life and the realization of everybody's creative potentialities held hegemony over the forces of repression, conformity and destructiveness. (Lawrence Friedman, *Lives of Erich Fromm* (xxxv))

> The Jew is a desert region, but underneath its thin layer of rock lies the molten lava of spirit and intellect. [Der Jude is ein wüste Gegend, unter deren dünner Gesteinschicht aber die feurig-flüssigen Massen des Geistigen liegen.]. (Ludwig Wittgenstein, 1931[1])

[1] In *Vermischte Bemerkungen*, ed. Georg Henrik von Wright in collaboration with Heikki Neiman (Frankfurt am Main: Suhrkamp, 1977); *Culture and Value*, rev ed. Alois Pichler, trans. Peter Winch (London: Wiley-Blackwell, 1998), 13.

A. Zakai, *Jewish Exiles' Psychological Interpretations of Nazism*,
https://doi.org/10.1007/978-3-030-54070-8_3

Erich Fromm (1900–1980) was a German-born American psychoanalyst, social philosopher, and sociologist, but above all a social critic who explored the interaction between psychology and society. By applying psychoanalytic principles to remedy cultural ills, he believed, mankind could develop a "sane society."[2] In *Escape from Freedom*, he explores humanity's shifting relationship with freedom, focusing on the psychological conditions that facilitated the rise of Nazism and Fascism.[3]

Fromm was born in Frankfurt am Main, the only child of Orthodox Jewish parents.[4] At the turn of the twentieth century Frankfurt was the financial capital of Germany, attracting Jewish business and intellectual ventures alongside those of other entrepreneurs. Fromm's father, Naphtali, was a wine merchant. The young Erich was strongly influenced by the Frankfurt Jewish community with its "medieval atmosphere, in which everything is dedicated to traditional learning."[5] His great uncle Ludwig Krause, a prominent Talmudic scholar, introduced Erich to the treasures and marvels of the Talmud and nurtured his appreciation of the contribution of his great-grandfather, Seligman Bär Bamberger, one of the leading German rabbinical scholars of the nineteenth century. The Talmud, which means *instruction and learning*, is a central text of Rabbinic Judaism. When Ludwig came to visit the family from Posen, which belonged to Prussia until 1919 and subsequently to Poland, he and Erich spent entire days studying Talmudic passages together. Erich became fascinated also with "the prophetic writings of Isaiah, Amos, and Hosea and their visions of peace and harmony among nations."[6]

World War I left a deep and indelible mark on Fromm. He remarked that it was "the most crucial experience in his life" and preoccupied his

[2] Froom, *The Sane Society* (New York: Henry Holt, 1955).

[3] I use the concepts Nazism and Fascism interchangeably, following Fromm, who wrote: "I use the term Fascism or authoritarianism to denote a dictatorial system of the type of German or Italian one. If I mean the German system in particular, I shall call it Nazism" (*Escape from Freedom*, 5, note 1).

[4] The following biography of Erich Fromm is based on several sources, including Friedman, *Lives of Erich Fromm*, and Guy Miron, "Judaism and Radical Thought – Erich Fromm and Leo Loewenthal during the Weimar Republic," MA Thesis, Hebrew University of Jerusalem, 1993 (in Hebrew). See also, Nathan Bamberger, "A Note on Erich Fromm's Rabbinical Roots," in *Tradition: A Journal of Orthodox Jewish Thought*, 29:3 (Spring 1995), pp. 52–4.

[5] Fromm, quoted in Friedman, *Lives of Erich Fromm*, 4.

[6] Ibid., 7.

thought and sensibilities.[7] Some of his uncles, cousins, and older schoolmates were among the fallen. At that time, Fromm came under the influence of Rabbi Nehemiah Nobel, the leader of Frankfurt's Orthodox Jewish community, who had a strong Hasidic bent. They spent hours together on the outskirts of Frankfurt discussing Nobel's sermons.[8] Through Nobel, Fromm became a Zionist, and his friends soon joined these meetings. Among them were Leo Löwenthal, the sociologist usually associated with the Frankfurt School; Ernst Simon, Jewish educator and religious philosopher; and philosopher of religion Franz Rosenzweig. The Nobel circle was instrumental in creating the Free Jewish Teaching Institute in Frankfurt, directed by Rosenzweig, in 1919.

Fromm began his studies at the University of Frankfurt am Main in 1918, but moved the following year to the University of Heidelberg, where he began studying sociology under Alfred Weber, brother of the famous sociologist Max Weber. Among his other teachers were the psychiatrist-philosopher Karl Jaspers and the Neo-Kantian philosopher Heinrich Rickert. From Weber, Fromm learned that the individual is inextricably rooted in the social and political life of his times. As he states in the foreword to *Escape from Freedom*,

> The basic entity of the social process is the individual, his desires and fears, his passions and reason, his propensities for good and for evil. To understand the dynamics of the social process we must understand the dynamics of the psychological processes operating within the individual, just as to understand the individual we must see him in the context of the culture which molds him. (viii)

Weber understood very early that Fromm was set on writing his dissertation on a Jewish topic and therefore allowed him to work on Jewish law—*halacha*, *halakhah*, or *halocho*—the accumulated corpus of Jewish religious laws derived from the written and oral Torah. The resulting *Jewish Law: A Contribution to the Study of Diaspora Judaism* addresses the

[7] Ibid., 9.

[8] On Rabbi Nobel, see Paul Mendes-Flohr, *Martin Buber: A Life of Faith and Dissent* (New Haven: Yale University Press, 2019). Buber too was deeply influenced by Hasidic lore. He viewed Hasidism as a source of cultural renewal for Judaism, frequently citing examples from the Hasidic tradition that emphasized community, interpersonal life, and finding meaning in common activities. He sought to reveal Hasidic texts "as unfettered teaching of mankind." See, Mendes-Flohr, *Martin Buber*, p. xv.

function of Jewish law in maintaining social cohesion and continuity in three communities: the Karaites, who adhere to the written Torah only; Reform Jews; and the Hasidim. During his years in Heidelberg, Fromm met almost daily with Salman Rabinkow, a Russian whose adherence to Habad Hasidism as well as to Marxist and socialist protest politics made a strong impression on him. Fromm would later remark that Rabinkow had influenced his "life more than any other man."[9]

Fromm was awarded his PhD in sociology from Heidelberg in 1922. He then trained in psychoanalysis at the University of Munich and the Berlin Psychoanalytic Institute and interned at Frieda Reichmann's sanatorium in Heidelberg. He and Frieda married in 1926, separated shortly thereafter, and divorced in 1942.

Fromm opened his own clinic in 1927 as a disciple of Sigmund Freud, but soon concluded that Freud's preoccupation with unconscious drives neglected the role of societal factors in human psychology. Based on what he had learned from Alfred Weber, he believed that an individual's personality was the product of culture as well as biology.

At that time, Fromm abandoned both traditional Jewish religious life and Zionism and adopted a more secular orientation. From 1927 to 1928 he and his colleagues at the Berlin Psychoanalytical Institute began a systematic synthesis of the theories of Marx and Freud. When Max Horkheimer became director of the Frankfurt Institute for Social Research (Institut für Sozialforschung), later known as the Frankfurt School, in 1930, Fromm helped to found the Frankfurt Psychoanalytic Institute. From 1929 to 1932, he taught there and at the University of Frankfurt and conducted research on the totalitarian disposition of the German workforce prior to Hitler's ascent to power. This work was published posthumously in 1984 as *The Working Class in Weimar Germany*.[10] He used the findings of this study in the chapter on the "Psychology of Nazism" in *Escape from Freedom*.

Following the Nazi Revolution of 1933, Fromm moved first to Geneva and within a year to Columbia University in New York City. In America he belonged to a Neo-Freudian school of psychoanalytical thought. After leaving Columbia in 1941, he helped to form the New York branch of the Washington School of Psychiatry in 1943, and in 1946 he co-founded the city's William Alanson White Institute of Psychiatry, Psychoanalysis, and

[9] Friedman, *Lives of Erich Fromm*, 16.
[10] Friedman, *Lives of Erich Fromm*, 39–45.

Psychology. He served on the faculty of Bennington College in Vermont from 1941 to 1949 and taught courses at the New School for Social Research in Manhattan from 1941 to 1959. Fromm developed a fruitful partnership with Karen Horney (1885–1952), a German psychoanalyst who practiced in the United States in her later career.[11] She worked on psychoanalytical theories; he, on various sociological models. More specifically, Horney was the first to recognize "the fundamental role of masochist strivings in the neurotic personality" (150–51), which informs the long chapter on "Mechanism of Escape" in *Escape from Freedom*. Horney's theories questioned some traditional Freudian views, particularly his theories of sexuality and instinct. She is credited with founding feminist psychology in response to Freud's theory of penis envy. Horney disagreed with him about differences between the psychology of men and women, attributing them to society and culture rather than biology.

Fromm moved to Mexico City in 1949 and in 1951 was appointed professor of psychoanalysis at the National Autonomous University of Mexico (UNAM). From 1957 to 1961, he held a concurrent professorship at Michigan State University and in 1962 had a similar arrangement as professor of psychiatry at New York University. In 1974 he moved from Mexico City to Muralto, Switzerland, and died there in 1980, five days before his eightieth birthday. Throughout his academic peregrinations, Fromm maintained a clinical practice and published eight books in German and 26 in English, five posthumously.

Fromm believed that an understanding of basic human needs is essential to understanding society and social behavior. He argued that social systems impede or preclude the satisfaction of different needs at the same time, thereby creating both individual psychological and wider societal conflicts. His first major work, *Escape from Freedom* (1941), traces the history of self-conscious liberty in the West from its awakening in the Middle Ages to its modern challenges. In *The Sane Society* (1955), he argues that consumer-oriented industrial society has alienated modern man from himself. Among his other books are *Man for Himself* (1947); *Psychoanalysis and Religion* (1950); the best-seller *The Art of Loving* (1956); *May Man Prevail?* (1961) with D.T. Suzuki and R. De Martino; *Beyond the Chains of Illusion* (1962); *The Revolution of Hope* (1968); and *The Crisis of Psychoanalysis* (1970).

[11] On Horney, see Dagmar Herzog, *Cold War Freud: Psychoanalysis in an Age of Catastrophe* (Cambridge: Cambridge University Press, 2017).

Escape from Freedom: Ideological and Historical Context

Escape from Freedom is the first of many studies written by intellectuals exiled from Nazi Germany that attempt to expose, explain, and counter the rise and triumph of Fascism in particular and the crisis of modern history in general. Eventually, these works would transform modern intellectual history. As a whole, both in form and content, they constitute a *Kulturkampf* against Nazi barbarism, attempting to rescue Western society from its menace through ferocious, indeed martial displays of these exiles' superior thinking and values.

Fromm declares in *Escape from Freedom* that "*the understanding of the reasons for the totalitarian flight from freedom is a premise for any action which aims at the victory over the totalitarian forces.*" He hopes that the book will "have a bearing on our course of action," (viii; emphasis added), believing, with Sir William Blackstone in his *Commentaries on the Laws of England*, 1765–1769, that *scribere est agere* [to write is to act].

Although he found refuge in the USA, Fromm never escaped the nightmares of Fascism and Nazism, which constantly stirred his soul, as evidenced by the speed at which he composed *Escape from Freedom* in little more than a year, only five years after his arrival in the New World. As a psychologist, he wrote, he felt he must "contribute to the understanding of the *present crisis* without delay" (vii; emphasis added). By the mid-1930s, "he had come to articulate the theoretical contours" of the book.[12] In 1939, he gave a colleague at Columbia a detailed outline and completed the manuscript in 1940. Clearly, Fromm felt he had a pressing idea that would elucidate the rise of Nazism and the atrocities of World War II. As he wrote, "the theme which is nearest to my heart and which is the leitmotif of the book is the problem of freedom and anxiety or the fear of freedom or the escape from freedom."[13] He sought to explore "the meaning of freedom for modern man," which "is crucial for the cultural and social *crisis* of our day" (vii; emphasis added). Crisis must lead to action. No wonder *Escape from Freedom* is considered a pillar of political psychology.

Based on the essential and inextricable connection between an individual's personality and the culture of his time, which he had learned from

[12] Friedman, *Lives of Erich Fromm*, 28.
[13] Ibid., 97.

his teacher Alfred Weber, Fromm argued that the "basic entity of the social process is the individual, his desire and fears, his passions and reason, his propensities for good and evil." To understand the social process, we must understand the psychological processes operating within individuals, and, conversely, to understand individuals, we must analyze the culture that shapes them. Based on these assumptions, the central, overarching argument of *Escape from Freedom* is:

> ... that modern man, freed from the bonds of pre-individualistic society, which simultaneously gave him security and limited him, has not gained freedom in the positive sense of the realization of his individual self; that is, the expression of his intellectual, emotional and sensuous potentialities. Freedom, though it has brought him independence and rationality, has made him isolated and, thereby, anxious and powerless. This isolation is unbearable and the alternatives he is confronted with are either escape from the burden of this freedom into a new dependence and submission, or to advance to the full realization of positive freedom which is based upon the uniqueness and individuality of man. (viii)

Modern man's isolation from society, becoming a negligible "atom" (238), and the doubts and fears that this process generates, explain how and why many seek the sanctuary and incentives of totalitarian societies.

Positive freedom means that man "can relate himself spontaneously to the world in love and work, in the genuine expression of his emotional, sensuous, and intellectual capacities." It "leads to happiness." The alternative course open to man is "to give up his freedom, and to try to overcome his aloneness by eliminating the gap that has arisen between his individual self and the world." This solution, argues Fromm, can be found "in all neurotic phenomena." More specifically, negative freedom means "to give up the independence of one's own individual self and to fuse one's self with somebody or something outside of oneself in order to acquire the strength which the individual self is lacking" (140–41). The result was that many in Germany were pulled toward Hitler and Nazism. While negative freedom symbolized "an inability to stand alone and to fully express" one's "own individual potentialities," positive freedom allows us to realize our "own spontaneous activity" (176–77).

In the final section of his book, "Freedom and Democracy," Fromm clarifies that he is dealing only "with one aspect of freedom: the powerlessness and insecurity of the isolated individual in modern society who has become free from all bonds that once gave meaning and security to life." The "individual cannot bear this isolation" because "he is utterly helpless in comparison with the world outside and deeply afraid of it." The result is that "the unity of the world has broken down for him and he has lost any point of orientation." Overcome by "doubts concerning himself, the meaning of life," he eventually loses "any principle according to which he can direct his actions." Paralyzed by his sense of helplessness, he is "*driven to bondage*." This new bondage differs "from the primary bonds" from which "he was not entirely separated," for the "*escape does not restore his lost security, but only helps him forget his self as a separate entity*." He finds only a "fragile security *at the expense of sacrificing the integrity of his individual self*." In sum, escape from freedom means that man "chooses to lose his self since he cannot bear to be alone. This freedom … leads into new bondage." (256–57; emphasis added).

It is intriguing to compare Fromm's views on positive and negative freedom to those of Martin Luther and Emanuel Kant with regard of the meaning and significance of freedom. According to Luther's famous saying in *On the Freedom of the Christian* (1520): "A Christian is a perfectly free lord of all, subject to none. A Christian is a perfectly dutiful servant of all, subject of all, subject to all." Kant too believed that freedom was essential to the human condition. In 1784 he coined the famous dictum: "Enlightenment is mankind's exit from its self-incurred immaturity. Immaturity is the inability to make use of one's own understanding without the guidance of another…. *Sapere Aude*! [dare to know] Have courage to use your own understanding! That is the motto of enlightenment."[14] Luther's context is the sacred drama of human salvation and redemption; Kant's context is the growth and power of human ability within a disenchanted world. And Fromm's context is that of the rise of fascism and Nazism.

Based on his training, Fromm psychoanalyzed contemporary fear of, and flight from, freedom by looking at, first, the emergence of the individual in Western culture and, second, the escape from freedom in his time. Clearly, he was not merely peering down from an ivory tower; Fromm believed that understanding the causes of the flight from freedom was a prerequisite for taking action to counter "*totalitarian forces*" (viii).

[14] See Kant, "What is Enlightenment?" in *What is Enlightenment? Eighteenth-Century Answers and Twentieth-Century Questions*, ed. James Schmidt (Berkeley: University of California Press, 1996), 58.

Escape from Freedom is a psychological analysis of the rise of individuation in Western culture and history. Its starting point is the Protestant Reformation: "The growing process of the emergence of the individual from its original ties, a process which we may call 'individuation' seems to have reached its peak in modern history in the centuries between the Reformation and the present." (24). Thus Luther in his *On the Freedom of the Christian* citing 1 Cor. ix. 19 asserts: "Though I be free from all men, yet have I made myself a servant unto all."

Fromm proceeds to claim that the Renaissance evidenced "the emergence of the individual in the modern sense" (45). He bases his argument on the Swiss historian Jacob Burckhardt's *The Civilization of the Renaissance in Italy* (*Die Kultur der Renaissance in Italien*, 1860), the theme of which is taken up by Hans Baron in *The Crisis of the Early Italian Renaissance*, another diatribe against Nazi barbarism penned by an exile from Nazi Germany. Baron argues that the Renaissance led to the rise of a "new civic philosophy" or a "new type of Humanism – Civic Humanism."[15]

Escape from Freedom: Content and Form

Escape from Freedom is a combative book: "If we want to fight Fascism we must understand it," Fromm declares (5). In direct response to the "[p]resent political developments and the dangers which they imply for the greatest achievements of modern culture—individuality and the uniqueness of personality," Fromm writes, he chose "to interrupt the work on the larger study"; namely, "the character structure of modern man and the problems of the interaction between psychological and sociological factors." Instead, the catastrophes threatening his beloved Western civilization drove him to "concentrate on one aspect of it which is crucial for the cultural and social crisis of our day: *the meaning of freedom for modern man*" (vii; emphasis added). He thus was one of the pioneers who used psychoanalysis in order to explain historical changes and transformations. The sociologist David Riesman, who underwent psychoanalysis by Fromm during the early and mid-1940s and later became a close friend of

[15] See *The Crisis of the Early Italian Renaissance: Civic Humanism and Republican Liberty in an Age of Classicism and Tyranny* (1955; Princeton: Princeton University Press, 1966), 459. See also Weinstein and Zakai, *Jewish Exiles and European Thought in the Shadow of the Third Reich*, chap. 1: "Hans Baron: Humanism and Republican Liberty in an Age of Tyranny" (Cambridge, UK: Cambridge University Press, 2017), 20–70.

his, was heavily influenced by Fromm's *Escape from Freedom*. In his highly influential book *The Lonely Crowd: A Study of the Changing Character of the American Character* (1950), he adopted Fromm's "application of a socially oriented psychoanalytic characterology to problems of historical changes."[16]

Among the various topics Fromm analyzes are "mechanisms of escape" and the psychological types of "the authoritarian character and the automaton," or the conformist character, essential to understanding Nazism and Fascism (207). The present crisis must be addressed because World War I "was regarded by many as the final struggle and … ultimate victory for freedom," yet "only a few years elapsed before new systems emerged which denied everything that men believed they had won in centuries of struggle." These systems "effectively took command of man's entire social and personal life" and effected "the submission of all but a handful of men to an authority over which they had no control" (4). *Escape from Freedom* seeks to explain why "millions in Germany were as eager to surrender their freedom as their fathers were to fight for it; that instead of wanting freedom, *they sought for ways of escape from it*; that other millions were indifferent and did not believe the defense of freedom to be worth fighting and dying for" (5; emphasis added).

Moreover, the crisis of democracy, of Fascism and Nazism, was not "a peculiar Italian or German problem, but one confronting every modern state" (5). Fromm quotes the American philosopher, psychologist, and educational reformer John Dewey (1859–1952), who asserted in *Freedom and Culture* (1939) that the "serious threat to our democracy is not the existence of foreign totalitarian states. It is the existence within our personal attitudes and within our institutions of conditions which have given a victory to external authority, discipline, uniformity and dependence upon The Leader." In other words, the "battlefield" is "within ourselves and our institutions."[17] Fromm, however, had a very different agenda from the atavistic one Dewey championed.

Fromm sought "to analyze those dynamic factors in the character structure of modern man, which made him want to give up freedom in Fascist countries and which so widely prevail in millions of our own people." Regrettably, he acknowledges, modern man conceives freedom in "the

[16] David Riesman, with Nathan Glazer and Reuek Denney, *The Lonely Crowd: A Study of the Changing American Character* (New Haven: Yale University Press, 1950), p. xiv.

[17] Dewey, *Freedom and Culture* (New York: G.P. Putnam's Sons, 1939), 49.

longing for submission, and the lust for power" (6). While political scientists and sociologists might identify rational motives for the rise of Nazism in certain well-constructed theories, the psychologist looks to irrational psychological factors: "we are dealing here with a political system which, essentially, does not appeal to rational forces of self-interest, but which arouses and mobilizes diabolic forces in man which we had believed to be nonexistent, or at least to have died out long ago" (6–7). Like Cassirer, Fromm uses the image of a volcano to describe the great upheavals of his time. Facing the grim consequence of Nazism's rise and triumph, Cassirer writes:

> In politics we are always living on *volcanic soil. We must be prepared for abrupt convulsions and eruptions.* In all critical moments of man's social life, the rational forces that resist the rise of the old mythical conceptions are no longer sure of themselves. In this moment the time of myth has come again. *For myth has not been really vanquished and subjugated. It is always there, lurking in the dark and waiting for its hour of opportunity.*[18]

Fromm argued that people had looked upon the periods before Nazism as "a volcano which for a long time has ceased to be a menace," but this complacency was shattered "when Fascism came into power" (8).

Fromm focuses on "what freedom means to modern man, and why and how he tries to escape from it." His premise is that "freedom characterizes human existence," but "its meaning changes according to the degree of man's awareness and conception of himself as an independent and separate being" (24). He finds the psychological starting-point in the period that witnessed the process of "individuation," or "the emergence of the individual from his original ties" (24), variously identified as the Reformation or the Renaissance. His analysis of "individuation" is based on the distinction between "positive" freedom, or "freedom to," and "negative" freedom, or "freedom from instinctual determination of his action" (32). Isaiah Berlin posits the same distinction; he follows the British tradition in defining "negative freedom" as freedom from interference, while "positive freedom," or self-mastery, asks not what we are free from, but what we are free to do. Berlin points out that these two conceptions can clash.[19] Well

[18] Cassirer, *The Myth of the State* (1946; New Haven: Yale University Press, 1967), 280; emphasis added.

[19] See "Two Concepts of Liberty" (1958), in Berlin, *Four Essays on Liberty* (Oxford: Oxford University Press, 1969).

before both Fromm and Berlin, the English philosopher T. H. Green (1836–1882) formulated this important distinction in 1880. He is commonly considered the father of modern reform liberalism and as the first major theorist to provide a philosophical grounding to what subsequently became the Labour Party in England and the Democratic Party of the New Deal and the Great Society in the United States.

Throughout his study, Fromm emphasizes the negative sense of "freedom from." In this context, he argues that the Protestant "Reformation is one root of the idea of human freedom and autonomy as it is represented in modern democracy" (38). In *The Protestant Ethic and the Spirit of Capitalism* (1905), Max Weber (1864–1920), the German sociologist, philosopher, jurist, and political economist who was the brother of Fromm's dissertation supervisor, proposed that ascetic Protestantism was one of the major "elective affinities" associated with the rise of market-driven capitalism and the rational-legal nation-state in the West. In clear contrast, Fromm argued that the Reformation stressed "the wickedness of human nature, the insignificance and powerlessness of the individual, and the necessity for the individual to subordinate himself to a power outside of himself." As such, "probably *no period since the sixteenth century … resembles ours as closely in regard to the ambiguous meaning of freedom*" (38; emphasis added).

Like Thomas Mann, who believed that the Protestant Reformation had signaled the beginning of the "secret union of the German spirit with the Demonic,"[20] Fromm read the course of German history in search of a singular turning-point toward the horrors of Nazism and Fascism and found that the Protestant Reformation's idea of the "unworthiness of the individual, his fundamental inability to rely on himself and his need to submit, *is also the main theme of Hitler's ideology*, which, however, lacks the emphasis on freedom and moral principles which was inherent in Protestantism" (38–39; emphasis added). Mann likewise rejected Weber's thesis linking the Protestant Reformation with the creation of the modern world, as can be seen in his novel *Doktor Faustus* (1947). According to Todd Kontje, "Mann's apocalyptic reading of German history traces a path from Luther and the Reformation to the smoking ruins of the

[20] "Germany and the Germans," in *Thomas Mann's Addresses Delivered at the Library of Congress, 1942–1949* (Washington, DC: Library of Congress, 1963), 51.

German cities and the gates of the concentration camps."[21] Their different historical contexts led Weber, Fromm, and Mann to offer radically different interpretations of the Protestant Reformation. Fromm found a close ideological affinity between the Reformation and Nazism; hence, for him "the study of the fifteenth and sixteenth centuries" served as "a particularly fruitful starting point for the understanding of the present scene" (39). What "characterized medieval in contrast to modern society is its lack of individual freedom" (41), yet this comparison is problematic because "medieval society did not deprive the individual of his freedom, because the 'individual' did not yet exist; man was still related to the world by primary ties" (43). Here, Fromm borrows Burckhardt's argument that in the Middle Ages, "man was conscious of himself only as a member of a race, people, party, family or corporation—only through some general category."[22]

The Renaissance, however, gave birth to the "rise in Italy of a powerful moneyed class the members of which were filled with a spirit of initiative, power, ambition." The result was nothing less than the "destruction of the medieval social structure" and "the emergence of the individual in the modern sense" (45). Again, this idea can be traced to Burckhardt, who claimed that, with the Renaissance, "man became a spiritual *individual*, and recognized himself as such."[23] Fromm used Burckhardt's contentions to advance his main thesis that "the destruction of the medieval world has taken four hundred years and is being completed in our era." The process of "human individuation, of the destruction of all 'primary bonds'" (237), led Fromm to conclude that man had "developed into being an 'atom'" (238).

Escape from Freedom is based on a very simple, uncritical, and uninformed glorification of mediaeval feudal society, which, Fromm seems to believe, was a kind of Golden Age or Eden, where human beings lived in harmony before the Fall, or the rise of capitalism in the early modern period. Cutting ties with tradition, Fromm believed, psychologically

[21] *Thomas Mann's World: Empire, Race, and the Jewish Question* (Ann Arbor: University of Michigan Press, 2011), 153. See also Zakai, "Apocalypse and Eschatology in Thomas Mann's *Doktor Faustus*: The 'Secret Union of the German Spirit with the Demonic,'" in Zakai, *The Pen Confronts the Sword: Exiled German Scholars Challenge Nazism* (Albany: SUNY Press, 2018).

[22] Burckhardt, *The Civilization of the Renaissance in Italy* (New York: Macmillan, 1921), 129.

[23] Ibid.

disrupted man's original sense of belonging and security in the world. Cast adrift and apparently blind to his extraordinary accomplishments and improved quality of life, man became prey to anxiety and longed for submission.

Freedom and the Protestant Reformation

The Renaissance provides the point of departure for Fromm's psychological analysis of the emergence of individuality in history. "We started with the discussion of the Renaissance because this period is the beginning of modern individualism," or "the emergence of man from a pre-individualistic existence to one in which he has full awareness of himself as a separate entity" (49).[24] Yet this new-found freedom also created "a deep feeling of insecurity, powerlessness, doubt, aloneness, and anxiety" (63).

In earlier times, the "medieval Church stressed the dignity of man, the freedom of his will, and the fact that his efforts were of avail; it stressed the likeness between God and man and also man's right to be confident of God's love" (73). However, following the Renaissance, the Protestant Reformation was the harbinger of "new religious doctrines" that were "an

[24] Finding the origins and sources of the rise of individualism, or individuation, in western history is admittedly a challenging task. Contrary to Fromm, Georg Wilhelm Friedrich Hegel (1770–1831) argued that the Homeric poems reveal "the free individuality of all the figures," and that "we meet … individuals" with a "wealth of particular traits" in "Homer's epic heroes." See Hegel, *Aesthetics: Lectures on Fine Art*, trans. T.M. Knox (Oxford: Clarendon, 1998), 2: 1053, 1178; and *Outlines of the Philosophy of Right*, trans. T.M. Knox (1821; Oxford: Oxford University Press, 2008), 321, where he asserts that "the principle of individuality arises" with the Greeks. Hegel furthermore maintained that the harmony of the social order "makes the Greek character into *beautiful individuality*, which is brought forth from spirit," quoted in Terry Pinkard, *Hegel's Phenomenology: The Sociability of Reason* (Cambridge: Cambridge University Press, 1994), 387, note 23; emphasis original. Elsewhere, Hegel inconsistently claims that "individuality emerges as the 'higher principle of modern times' in the way in which individuals 'return back fully to themselves,'" which, as he noted, "contrasted modern life with ancient Greek [life]." See Pinkard, *Hegel: A Biography* (Cambridge: Cambridge University Press, 2001), 196. In a dissenting view, the Hungarian Marxist philosopher, aesthetician, literary historian, and critic Georg Lukács (1885–1971) argued that the individual in Homer's epic works, the "epic hero is, strictly speaking, never an individual" (*The Theory of the Novel: A Historic-philosophical Essay on the Forms of Great Epic Literature* [1920; London: Merlin, 1971], 66). Likewise, the German-Jewish philologist and comparative literary critic Erich Auerbach (1892–1957) argued that Homeric characters lack a "distinct stamp of individuality" (*Mimesis: The Representation of Reality in Western Literature* [1946; Princeton: Princeton University Press, 2003], 18).

answer to psychic needs which in themselves were brought about by *the collapse of the medieval system* and by the beginnings of capitalism" (103; emphasis added). This interpretation was largely influenced by two classic works, *The Protestant Ethic and the Spirit of Capitalism*, in which Max Weber posits that Calvinist ethics and ideas influenced the development of capitalism; and *Religion and the Rise of Capitalism* by Richard Henry Tawney (1880–1962), the English economic historian, social critic, and ethical and Christian socialist, who explored the relationship between Protestantism and economic development in the sixteenth and seventeenth centuries.[25] Tawney bemoaned the division between commerce and social morality brought about by the Protestant Reformation, which subordinated Christian teaching to the pursuit of material wealth. Fromm drew from and criticized both these works.

According to Fromm's psychological reading, Luther's system assumed the existence of "an innate evilness in man's nature," and he cites Luther's contention that Man has an evil and vicious nature: "'*naturaliter et inevitabiliter mala et vitiata natura.*'" From this "conviction of man's rottenness and powerlessness to do anything good on his own merits" followed the existential sense of insecurity with regard to salvation (74–75). Paradoxically, if "Luther freed people from the authority of the Church, he made them submit to a much more tyrannical authority, that of a God who insisted on complete submission of man and the annihilation of the individual self as the essential condition to his salvation." No one can overlook the striking resemblance between Luther's teaching and Nazism: "*Luther's 'faith' was the conviction of being loved upon the condition of surrender*, a solution which has much in common with the principle of complete submission of the individual to the state and the 'leader'" (81;emphasis original). Fromm is constantly and eagerly reading history through the lens of the German crisis of his times.

Like Luther, Calvin contributed to human anxiety and doubt. His concept of predestination was likewise "rooted in the powerlessness of man; self-humiliation and the destruction of human pride are the *Leitmotiv* of his whole thinking. Only he who despises this world can devote himself to the preparation for the future world" (84; emphasis original). This thesis differed radically from the understandings of "Augustine, Aquinas and

[25] *The Protestant Ethic and the Spirit of Capitalism*, trans. Talcott Parsons (1905; London: George Allen & Unwin, Ltd., 1930); *Religion and the Rise of Capitalism: A Historical Study* (London: John Murray, 1926).

Luther," since Calvin made predestination "the central doctrine" of "his whole system. He gives it a new version by assuming that God not only predestines some for grace, but decides that others are destined for eternal damnation" (87). With Calvin, God's love is replaced by God's enmity. Fromm was quick to point out the resemblance between Calvin's theory of predestination and Nazi thought, arguing that "one implication ... should be explicitly mentioned here, since *it has found its most vigorous revival in Nazi ideology*"; namely "the principle of the basic inequality of men" (89; emphasis added), which denied any possibility of human solidarity. The Genevan reformer envisaged only two kinds of people: "those who are saved and those who are destined to eternal damnation." With Nazism, the doctrine that men are basically "unequal according to their racial background is a confirmation of the same principle with a different rationalization" (89–90).

Luther and Calvin's teachings were based on an "all-pervading hostility." Both belonged to "the ranks of the greatest haters among the leading figures in history, certainly among religious leaders." The core of their inherent hostility derives from their concept of God, especially Calvin's God, who is "arbitrary and merciless" and "destined part of mankind to eternal damnation without any justification or reason except that this act was an expression of God's power" (95–96). In Marxist terms, argued Fromm, the middle class reflects this hostility and resentment in its "moral indignation, which has invariably been characteristic of the lower middle class from Luther's time to Hitler's." Simply put, the middle class was "envious of those who had wealth and power and could enjoy life" and "rationalized this resentment and envy of life in terms of moral indignation and in the conviction that these superior people would be punished by eternal suffering" (96).

Fromm's reading of the Reformation clearly draws on the German middle class's role in the rise and triumph of Nazism. His model was rests upon the findings of an unpublished sociological study, "The Character of German Workers and Employees in 1929/30," which he conducted with three colleagues (212). He argued that the reason "why the Nazi ideology was so appealing to the lower middle class has to be sought in the social character of the lower middle class." It was "the lower strata of the middle class, composed of small shopkeepers, artisans, and white-color workers," whose "outlook on life was narrow" and who "suspected and hated the stranger" (211–12). Hitler was "the typical representative of the lower middle class, a nobody with no chances or future," who "felt very intensely the role of being an outcast," as clearly revealed in his autobiographical rant *Mein Kampf* (217).[26]

More than anything else, Fromm emphasized, "the breakdown of the medieval system of society had one main significance for all classes of society: the individual was left alone and isolated." Indeed, he was "free," but this freedom was a double-edged sword:

> Man was deprived of security he had enjoyed, of the unquestionable feeling of belonging, and he was torn loose from the world which had satisfied his quest for security both economically and spiritually. He felt alone and anxious. But he was free to act and to think independently, to become his own master and to do with his life as he could—not as he was told to do. (99)

Faithful to his Marxist historical materialism, Fromm argued that only the rich could "enjoy the fruits of the new freedom" and "the positive meaning of freedom was dominant for the new capitalist" (99). However, for the middle class freedom "brought isolation and personal insignificance more than strength and confidence" (100). In German society, this process had terrible consequences: the middle class welcomed the rise of Nazism after defeat in World War I. At that time, the "vast majority of the population was seized with the feeling of individual insignificance and powerlessness" (217), a psychological dynamic that "Nazism resurrected" (221). The Reformation thus led directly to the rise of Nazism, a thesis that Thomas Mann constructed in *Doktor Faustus* for very different reasons.

Fromm's psychological reading and explanation of history is based on his traumatic experience during the rise of Nazism and Fascism. Evidently, the middle class experience in democratic states like the United States and England was radically different from that in modern Germany. Fromm was a prisoner in the citadel of his own Marxist ideology and interpretation, which led him to stress the crucial role of the rise or the frustrations

[26] Thomas Mann fiercely mocked Hitler's character: "The fellow is a catastrophe. But that is no reason why we should not find him interesting, as a character and an event. Consider the circumstances. Here is a man possessed of a bottomless resentment and a festering desire for revenge; a man ten times a failure, extremely lazy, incapable of steady work; a man who has spent long periods in institutions; a disappointed bohemian artist; a total good-for-nothing." See "Bruder Hitler," *Esquire*, 11, n. 3 (1939); http://larvatus.livejournal.com/291296.html; and"ABrother," in *Thomas Mann: Death in Venice, Tonio Kröger, and Other Writings* (New York: Continuum, 1939), 298.

of the middle class, or the bourgeoisie, during the early modern period in supporting the Nazi Revolution. As the French philosopher, anthropologist, and sociologist Bruno Latour writes, "we are always prisoners of language";[27] or in other words, we are always prisoners of our culture, our ideologies, and our discourse.

Fromm claimed that "for great parts of the lower middle class in Germany and other European countries, the sado-masochistic is typical"; it was "this kind of character structure to which Nazi ideology had its strongest appeal" (163–64). Moreover, the "destructiveness in the lower middle class" is responsible for "the isolation of the individual and the suppression of individual expansiveness" (184–85). Instead of basing his life on positive freedom, the individual is directed by negative freedom: he "ceases to be himself" and rather "adopts entirely the kind of personality offered to him by cultural patterns." In sum, his "automaton conformity" threw up the stiff-armed salute to Nazi and Fascist regimes (185–86).

Freedom and Modern Man

> Our aim [is] to show that the structure of modern society affected man in two ways simultaneously: he becomes more isolated, self-reliant, and critical, and he becomes more isolated, alone, and afraid. (Fromm, *Escape from Freedom* (124))

The overarching thesis of *Escape from Freedom* is that from the time of the Renaissance, the Protestant Reformation, and the beginnings of capitalism, "freedom *from* traditional bonds of medieval society, though giving the individual a new feeling of independence, at the same time made him feel alone and isolated, filled him with doubt and anxiety, and drove him into new submission and into a compulsive and irrational activity" (103; emphasis original). Later, the development of capitalist society "affected personality in the same direction" and "in two ways simultaneously: [man] becomes more independent, self-reliant, and critical, and he becomes more isolated, alone, and afraid" (104).

Fromm's criticism of modern capitalist society resembles that of Horkheimer and Adorno in *Dialectic of Enlightenment*. He speaks of "the negative side of freedom, the burden which it puts on man." Paradoxically,

[27] Bruno Latour, "Why Has Critique Run Out of Steam? From Matters of Fact to Matters of Concern," *Critical Inquiry*, 30 (Winter 2004): 227.

he argues, "although man has rid himself from old enemies of freedom, new enemies of a different nature have arisen: enemies which are not essentially external restraints, but *internal factors blocking full realization of the freedom of personality*" (104; emphasis added). Likewise, the authors of *Dialectic of Enlightenment* argue that originally, the "Enlightenment, understood in the widest sense as the advance of thought, has always aimed at liberating human beings from fear and installing them as masters." Its "program was the disenchantment of the world" and its charge to "dispel myths, to overthrow fantasy with knowledge." However, with the rise of Fascism and National Socialism, reason seemed to collapse; discourse regressed into superstition and myth. Hence, they sought "to explain why humanity, instead of entering a truly human state, is sinking into a new kind of barbarism," leading to the "reversion of enlightened civilization to barbarism in reality."[28] Exiled representatives of the Frankfurt School of social theory and philosophy thus reached the same conclusions regarding the decline of freedom and reason in contemporary history.

While Fromm argued that capitalist society impeded the "full realization of the freedom of personality," Horkheimer and Adorno regarded class struggle in modern capitalist society in terms of Hobbes's war of all against all, or the law of the jungle. Self-preservation became the source and thrust of all human action: "Spinoza's proposition: 'the endeavor of preserving oneself is the first and only basis of virtue,' contains the true maxim of all Western civilization." Inextricably linked to the Age of Reason and the Enlightenment, capitalism institutionalizes "the process of self-preservation" in "the bourgeois division of labor."[29] Fromm focuses on the inner abysses of the human soul and spirit; Horkheimer and Adorno on the horrifying consequences of capitalist society.

According to Fromm, freedom of speech, for example, once meant "freedom from external authorities," but is now suppressed by "inner restraints, compulsions, and fears, which tend to undermine the meaning of the victories freedom has won against its traditional enemies" (105). Instead, we should strive toward "*a new kind of freedom, one which enables*

[28] Horkheimer and Adorno, *Dialectic of Enlightenment: Philosophical Fragments*, ed. Gunzelin Schmid Noerr, trans. Edmund Jephcott (Stanford, CA: Stanford University Press, 2002), i, xiv, xix. An analysis of the content and form of this study can be found in my book, *The Pen Confronts the Sword*, chap. 4, "Enlightenment and Its Enemies: The Dialectic of *Dialectic of Enlightenment*."

[29] Horkheimer and Adorno, *Dialectic of Enlightenment*, 22–23.

us to realize our own individual self, to have faith in this self and in life"; he calls this freedom positive, or "freedom to" (106; emphasis added). Beyond the inner, psychological dimension, the "peak in the evolution of freedom" was "the modern democratic state based on the principle of equality of all men and the equal right of everybody to share in the government by representatives of his choice" (107). Ernst Cassirer shared this view, arguing in Hegelian terms in *The Myth of the State* that concepts determine the structure of reality; hence, during the Age of Enlightenment, "reason had first declared its power and its claim to rule the social life of man. It had emancipated itself from the guardianship of theological thought; it could stand on its own."[30] Cassirer found evidence to support his argument in the US Declaration of Independence and, later, the French Declaration of the Rights of Man and the Citizen (*Déclaration des droits de l'homme et du citoyen*, 1789).

Eventually, while capitalism "contributed tremendously to the increasing of positive freedom, to the growth of an active, critical, responsible self," it made "the individual more alone and isolated and imbued him with a feeling of insignificance and powerlessness" (108). The theology of Luther and Calvin had psychologically prepared man for the role he was required to assume in modern society: "of feeling his own self to be insignificant and of being ready to *subordinate his life exclusively for purposes which were not his own*." The outcome of this psychological willingness "to become nothing but the means for the glory of a God who represented neither justice nor love" was a readiness "*to accept the role of a servant to the economic machine*" of capitalism "*and eventually a 'Führer'*" in Nazi Germany (111; emphasis added). Fromm turned Weber's and Tawney's thesis upside down.

Freedom and Democracy

Beyond the role of capitalism in ensuring human servitude, Fromm emphasizes that the "principal social avenues of escape in our times are the submission to a leader, as has happened in Fascist countries, and the compulsive conforming as is prevalent in our own democracy" (134). In the final chapter of *Escape from Freedom*, titled "Freedom and Democracy," he combines sociological and psychological approaches.

[30] Cassirer, *Myth of the State*, 167.

> In discussing the two aspects of freedom for modern man, we have pointed out the economic conditions that make for increasing isolation and powerlessness of the individual in our era; in discussing the psychological results we have shown that this powerlessness leads either to the kind of escape that we find in the authoritarian character, or else to a compulsive conforming in the process of which the isolated individual becomes an automaton, loses his self, and yet at the same time consciously conceives of himself as free and subject only to himself. (241)

Modern capitalist society projects "the illusion of individuality."[31] Its power to foster conformity can be found, for example, in education, which too often leads to "elimination of spontaneity" and "the substitution of original psychic acts by superimposed feelings, thoughts, and wishes" (242). Horkheimer and Adorno lodge the same criticism, asserting that "modern capitalist mass culture, the entertainment industry, especially cinema, radio, jazz, and magazines," as well as advertising, provide clear evidence of the inherent "rationality of domination."[32]

Likewise with regard to spontaneity: negative freedom, "freedom from," brings with it a new bondage. The escape from freedom "only helps" man "to forget his self as a separate entity. He finds new and fragile security at the expense of sacrificing the integrity of his individual self. He chooses to lose his self since he cannot bear to be alone. Thus freedom—as freedom from—leads into new bondage" (256–57). Nevertheless, the possibility of "a state of positive freedom in which the individual exists as an independent self and yet is not isolated but united with the world, with other men, and nature" persists. Man can achieve it "by realization of his self, by being himself." (257).

Contrary to idealist philosophers like Kant, who believed that self-realization can be achieved by intellectual insight alone, Fromm declares:

> We believe that the realization of the self is accomplished not only by an act of thinking but also by the realization of man's total personality, by an active expression of his emotional and intellectual potentialities. These potentialities are present in everybody; they become real only to the extent to which they are expressed. In other words, *positive freedom consists in the spontaneous activity of the total, integrated personality.* (258; emphasis original)

[31] Compare "free and subject only to himself" to Martin Luther's assertion that "A Christian is a perfectly free lord of all, subject to none," in "On Christian Freedom" (1520).

[32] Horkheimer and Adorno, *Dialectic of Enlightenment*, 95.

Spontaneous activity means that man cannot live compulsively or automatically. Above all, it means that he is "aware of himself as an active and creative individual and recognizes that *there is only one meaning of life: the act of living itself*" (263; emphasis original).

Fromm's strong focus on the psychological aspect of freedom did not hinder him from understanding that "psychological problems cannot be separated from the material basis of human existence," or from the economic, social, and political structure of society. Realizing positive freedom and individualism is "also bound up with economic and social changes that will permit the individual to become free in terms of the realization of his self" (271). In this broad context, he stresses the difference between democracy and Fascism, thus returning full circle to the beginning of his book. Now, he contends, "Democracy is a system that creates the economic, political, and cultural conditions for the full development of the individual. Fascism is a system that, regardless under which name, *makes the individual subordinate to extraneous purposes and weakens the development of genuine individuality*" (274; emphasis added). Thus, he concludes his highly popular defense of liberal democracy from the psychological and Marxist perspectives. *Escape from Freedom* is a timeless classic because it not only examines the psychological roots of Nazism and Fascism in Europe, but also demonstrates how economic and social restraint can lead to authoritarianism anywhere.

Siegfried Kracauer's *From Caligari to Hitler*: Weimar Cinema as Pandora's Box

Siegfried Kracauer (1889–1966), was a German writer, journalist, sociologist, cultural critic, and film theorist. In his book, *From Caligari to Hitler: A Psychological History of the German Film* (1947), he discovered a latent diabolic strain in the German soul that emerged after World War I.

The book proposed a link between the apolitical and escapist orientation of Weimar-era cinema and the totalitarianism that followed. The Weimar films presaged the coming of the Nazi state's hell on earth. They were reminiscent of Pandora's box—out of which flew a multitude of unforeseen evils and travails—and as in Greek tragedy, prophetic visions of doom and calamity announced in the first act came to their horrifying, devastating culmination in the final act, the Nazi state.

Introduction

> It is my contention that through an analysis of the German films deep psychological dispositions predominant in Germany from 1918 to 1933 can be exposed – dispositions which influenced the course of events and which will have to be reckoned with in the post-Hitler era. (Siegfried Kracauer, *From Caligari to Hitler* (1947), li)

Kracauer was a stern critic of Germany; he saw that defeat in World War I had utterly unmoored its people from reality. His book, *From Caligari to*

A. Zakai, *Jewish Exiles' Psychological Interpretations of Nazism*,
https://doi.org/10.1007/978-3-030-54070-8_4

Hitler: A Psychological History of the German Film,[1] is a painful, vivid, first-hand commentary on the tortured German soul, staggering between diabolic tyranny and chaos, a struggle that culminated in the rise and triumph of Nazism. The title implies that the apparitions, insanity, terror, and dread of impending disaster so prevalent on the German screen during the Weimar Republic were fully realized in the Nazi regime. The argument proceeds in four well-defined acts: the Archaic Period (1895–1918), when a national cinema began to emerge, the Postwar Period (1918–1924), when diabolic characters in the movies announced the birth of terrible, antic portents in the German soul; the Stabilized Period (1924–1929), when German society was in a state of paralysis and proved unable to work out its problems; and the Pre-Hitler Period (1929–1933), marked by unmistakable signs of widespread despair, and paving the way for the Nazi revolution and the Nazi state. Prophetic visions of doom and devastation that first appeared on the postwar screen became real under the Nazis. Kracauer's analysis exposes the psychological dispositions predominant in Germany from 1918 to 1933 that influenced the course of events during the Weimar Republic. The author proposes an inextricable connection between history and the movies and *vice versa*.

From Caligari to Hitler resembles Dante's *Inferno*: an author's long, painful wandering into the abyss. However, in Dante, the epic journey to the very bottom of hell precedes ascent and victory, while Kracauer sees no triumph, only defeat and calamity. The poet Virgil guides Dante out of hell; in Kracauer's rendering, the Germans themselves have created their *Inferno* on earth, and rather than leading them out of it, Hitler drew them deeper and deeper into the darkest abyss. Kracauer's study also resembles John Milton's *Paradise Lost*, in which Satan, the fallen Angel, becomes a hero; but Kracauer can envision no *Paradise Regained*, no redemption for Germany's fall into the hands of Hitler. Above all, Kracauer's book resembles Thomas Mann's *Doctor Faus*tus, which identifies the Nazi state with hell, yet Kracauer identifies the rise of the diabolic element latent in the German soul at a far earlier time, directly after World War I. *From Caligari to Hitler* may rightly be seen as a preface or an introduction to *Doctor Faustus*.

[1] Siegfried Kracauer, *From Caligari to Hitler: A Psychological History of the German Film* (1947; Princeton: Princeton University Press, 2004). All references in the text are to this edition.

Along with film critic Harry Alan Potamkin (1900–1933), Kracauer firmly believed that German film constituted a historical "German document" (228). From *The Cabinet of Dr. Caligari* (1920) to *The Last Will of Dr. Mabuse* (1933), cinema embodied the satanic and demonic themes ingrained in the German soul and imagination; Kracauer saw these films as "anticipations of the spell that Hitler was to cast on the German people."[2] Given the great influence of *The Cabinet of Dr. Caligari*, Kracauer characterized the entire period between 1918 to 1933 as a journey from the horrors of Caligari to the terrors of Hitler, and his book echoes the film's intense foreboding and sense of determinism. In sociological terms, he emphasized the rule of the middle class during the Weimar Republic; the screen, he argued, opened a window onto the soul of the people who would eventually succumb to Nazism. Other contemporary works that focused on the crucial role of the middle class in facilitating Hitler's rise to power include Erich Fromm's *Escape from Freedom* (1941) and Max Horkheimer and Theodore Adorno's *Dialectic of Enlightenment* (1944).

Kracauer's *From Caligari to Hitler* considers the history and psychology of the Nazi regime writ large. The book reads like a horror movie, portraying a series of German films in which the boundaries between the real and the unreal are abolished; shock, panic, sadism, depravity, tyranny, authoritarianism, lawlessness, anarchy, and insanity reign; a dread of ever-impending doom, ominous foreboding, and terror of judgment and punishment haunt everyone; disaster hovers; and all these elements reflect the "German imagination," the "German mind," or the "German soul" in its flight from reason and reality. Replete with horror and dread of frightening omens, Kracauer's book clearly recalls the words inscribed above the gates of hell in Dante's *Inferno*: "Abandon all hope, ye who enter here." Kracauer saw no hope of derailing the impending triumph of Nazism. He had lived in Germany long enough to understand the signs:

> Nazism taught the Germans to see themselves as a beleaguered nation, constantly set upon by enemies external and internal. Metaphors of infection and disease, of betrayal and stabs in the back, were central to Nazi discourse. The concentration camp became the place where those metaphorical evils could be rendered concrete and visible. Here, behind the barbed wire, were

[2] Thomas Elsaesser, *Weimar Cinema and After: Germany's Historical Imaginary* (London and New York: Routledge, 2000), 61–62.

> the traitors, Bolsheviks, parasites, and Jews who were intent on destroying the Fatherland.[3]

In face of the horrifying phenomenon of Nazism, Kracauer developed his own prophetic, apocalyptic, and eschatological mode of historical thought and exegesis, precisely like Mann's in *Doctor Faustus*.[4] Kracauer focuses on the characters and events in the Weimar films that prefigured real historical characters and events under Nazism. In the Nazi regime, "Caligaris hypnotized innumerable Cesares into murder" (272); in the 1934 Nazi Party Congress in "Nuremberg, the ornamental patterns of *Nibelungen* appeared on gigantic scale" (272); and in *The Last Will of Dr. Mabuse* (1933), Fritz Lang "resuscitated his super criminal to mirror the obvious … traits of Hitler" (84). The Nazi regime fully incarnated and facilitated the horror and terror portrayed on the Weimar screen; omens in the films were realized in the Nazi state.

A book about Dr. Caligari must bear his mark. Like these movies, Kracauer depicted "[t]he German soul, haunted by the alternative images of tyrannic rule and instinct-governed chaos, threatened by doom on either side, tossed about in gloomy space like the phantom ship in *Nosferatu*" (107). However, he traces the satanic, demonic dimension in the German soul only to the trauma of defeat in World War I. Nowhere in the book does he allude to its earlier sources and origins. Mann found these in the old legend of Faustus, and his novel *Doctor Faustus* traces a direct path from "Luther and the Reformation to the smoking ruins of the German cities and the gates of the concentration camps."[5] Georg Lukács saw the "danger of a barbaric underworld latent in German civilization as its necessary complementary product."[6] Ernst Cassirer identified the twentieth-century myths of the race, the hero, and the state. He remarked:

[3] Adam Kirsch, "The System: Two New Histories Show How the Nazi Concentration Camps Worked," *New Yorker* (6 April 2015): 80–81.

[4] For an analysis of Mann's *Doctor Faustus*, see Avihu Zakai, "Apocalypse and Eschatology in Thomas Mann's *Doctor Faustus*: The Secret Union of the German Spirit with the Demonic," in *The Pen Confronts the Sword: Exiled German Scholars Challenge Nazism* (Albany: SUNY, 2018), 23–82.

[5] Todd Kontje, *Thomas Mann's World: Empire, Race, and the Jewish Question* (Ann Arbor: University of Michigan Press, 2011), 153.

[6] Thomas Reed, *Thomas Mann: The Uses of Tradition* (1973; Oxford: Clarendon, 1996), 385.

"In politics we are always living on a *volcanic soil and must be prepared for sudden convulsions and eruptions.*"[7]

In Kracauer's interpretation, Germans increasingly turned to the movies after World War I because they gratified their psychological urge to escape from reality. They did not escape into the Keystone Cops or Buster Keaton or the Little Tramp; *Caligari*'s dark themes struck a deep chord; it was the "archetype of all forthcoming postwar film" (3). Kracauer lived in Weimar Germany and saw many of the movies he wrote about when they were first released; and although he wrote it in the United States in the early 1940s, his study bears living witness to their reception. He foresaw how the tragedy of German history would unfold: from Dr. Caligari, not from Goethe and Schiller, whose eighteenth-century Weimar Classicism (*Weimarer Klassik*) proposed a new humanism synthesizing Classical, Enlightenment, and Romantic ideas.

D. H. Lawrence's remarkable "Letter from Germany," written in 1928 and published in 1934, noted the barbaric turn during the Weimar Republic, "whirling to the ghost of the old Middle Ages of Germany, then to the Roman days, then to the days of the silent forest and the dangerous, lurking barbarians." In sum, "[s]omething about the Germanic races is unalterable. White-skinned, elemental, and dangerous."[8] Kracauer strove to expose this very same barbaric turn through the medium of films in *From Caligari to Hitler.*

Biographical Sketch

> ... a sort of joylessness hovered over his own milieu, despite its humane scholarly tradition. (Theodore Adorno, "The Curious Realist: On Siegfried Kracauer" (1964))

Kracauer was born into a Jewish family in Frankfurt am Main in 1889.[9] He graduated from high school in 1907 and studied architecture at Darmstadt University of Technology from 1907 to 1913, earning a doctorate in

[7] Cassirer, *The Myth of the State* (1946; New Haven: Yale University Press, 1967), 280.

[8] Reed, *Thomas Mann*, 399, note 88. See also, "D. H. Lawrence: A Letter from Germany," at http://www.newstatesman.com/europe/2013/07/d-h-lawrence-letter-germany/

[9] On Kracauer's life and thought, see Koch, *Siegfried Kracauer*; Johannes von Moltke, *The Curious Humanist: Siegfried Kracauer in America* (Oakland: University of California Press, 2016); and Dagmar Barnouw, *Critical Realism: History, Photography, and the Works of Siegfried Kracauer* (Baltimore: Johns Hopkins University, 1994.)

engineering in 1914.[10] He worked as an architect until 1920. Toward the end of the First World War he befriended and became an early philosophical mentor to the young Adorno, who later recalled Kracauer's important influence on him:

> For years Siegfried Kracauer read the *Critique of Pure Reason* regularly on Saturday afternoon with me. I am not exaggerating in the slightest when I say that I owe more to this reading than to my academic teachers. ... If in my later reading of traditional philosophical texts I was not so much impressed with their unity and systematic consistency as I was concerned with the play of forces at work under the surface of every closed doctrine and viewed the codified philosophies as force fields in each case, it was certainly Kracauer who impelled me to do so.[11]

With Kracauer, Adorno "perceived for the first time the expressive moment in philosophy: putting into words the thoughts that come into one's head."[12]

From 1922 to 1933, Kracauer worked for the *Frankfurter Zeitung*, first as its film critic in Frankfurt and then, beginning in 1930, as the cultural editor of the paper's Berlin bureau. The paper was an important mouthpiece for the liberal bourgeois extra-parliamentary opposition. As one of the few democratic papers during the Weimar Republic, it was treated with hostility and derision by nationalist circles, especially for its unequivocal support of the Treaty of Versailles (1919). The Weimar Republic has sometimes been described as a *Republik ohne Republikaner* (a republic without republicans); it was a weak regime, unable to withstand antidemocratic tendencies on the right and on the left.

In Frankfurt, Kracauer worked alongside the renowned cultural critic Walter Benjamin (1892–1940) and the Marxist philosopher Ernst Bloch (1885–1977), and in a 1928 essay he wrote what would become the leitmotiv of *From Caligari to Hitler*: "Films do not cease to reflect society. On the contrary: the more incorrectly they present the surface of things, the more correct they become and the more clearly they mirror the secret

[10] Esther Leslie, "Siegfried Kracauer and Walter Benjamin," in *Memory: Histories, Theories, Debates*, ed. Susannah Radstone and Bill Schwarz (New York: Fordham University Press, 2010), 124.

[11] Adorno and Nicholsen, "Curious Realist," 160. See also Adorno, *Notes to Literature*, ed. Rolf Tiedemann (New York: Columbia University Press, 1992), 2:58.

[12] Adorno, *Notes to Literature*, 59.

mechanisms of society."[13] A historian claimed that Kracauer's film criticism functioned as a "diagnosis of his age."[14]

Between 1923 and 1925, he wrote an essay entitled "Der Detektiv-Roman" ("The Detective Novel") about the meaning of everyday phenomena in modern society. He continued to explore this theme over the next few years, constructing theoretical methods used to analyze photography, films, dance, Kafka, the Bible, bestsellers and their readers, circuses, advertising, tourism, hotel lobbies, shopping arcades, city planning, and boredom. He published these pieces in the 1927 collection *Ornament der Masse* (*The Mass Ornament*), which describes the tastes, amusements, and everyday lives of the general population and takes up such themes as urban culture, isolation and alienation, and the relation between the group and the individual. For Kracauer, the most revelatory facets of modern life in the West lay on the surface, in the ephemeral and the marginal. He was especially fascinated by the United States of America, where he eventually settled after fleeing Germany. He saw its culture as defined almost exclusively by the ostentatious display of surface.

After reading *The Mass Ornament*, Adorno wrote to Kracauer in 1933, remarking that he was "the first of us all to tackle afresh the problems of the Enlightenment." German historian Inka Mülder-Bach argued that in retrospect, the work "reads like a nucleus of *Dialectic of Enlightenment*," Max Horkheimer and Theodor Adorno's celebrated book. However, in 1927 Kracauer had not "lost faith in the possibility of historical progress,"[15] whereas Horkheimer and Adorno, writing during World War II and the horrors of the Holocaust, had lost faith in the Enlightenment.[16] As Jürgen Habermas wrote: "In their blackest book, *Dialectic of Enlightenment*, Horkheimer and Adorno [conceptualize] the Enlightenment's process of self-destruction. On their analysis, it is no longer possible to place hope in the liberating force of Enlightenment."[17]

[13] Kracauer, quoted in Elsaesser, *Weimar Cinema*, 98.

[14] Koch, *Siegfried Kracauer*, 45.

[15] Adorno, quoted by Inka Mülder-Bach, "Introduction," in Kracauer, *The Salaried Masses: Duty and Distraction in Weimar Germany*, trans. Quintin Hoare (1930; Verso: London, 1998), 12.

[16] For an analysis of *Dialectic of Enlightenment*, see Avihu Zakai, *Pen Confronts the Sword*, chap. 4: "Enlightenment and Its Enemies: Max Horkheimer and Theodor Adorno and the Dialectic of *Dialectic of Enlightenment*," 243–306.

[17] Jürgen Habermas, *The Philosophical Discourse of Modernity: Twelve Lectures*, trans. F.G. Lawrence (Cambridge, MA: MIT Press, 1993), 106. See also Jeffrey Herf, "Dialectic of Enlightenment Reconsidered," *New German Critique*, 117 (fall 2012): 81–89.

Nonetheless, the works share a close affinity in their determinist teleology; all three authors believed that crisis determines the course and progress of history. Kracauer argued that since Nazi Germany "carried out what had been anticipated by her cinema from its very beginning, conspicuous screen characters now came true in life itself" (272). They all regarded Nazism as the *terminus ad quem*—the end, the *telos*, to which history had turned; hence, their studies strove to explain the course of history, German history above all, according to this horrifying end.

In 1930, Kracauer published *Die Angestellten* (*The Salaried Masses*), another collection of pieces published previously in the *Frankfurter Zeitung*, in which he cited conversations, newspaper articles, advertisements, and personal correspondence to chart the bland horror of the everyday in Weimar's cities, arguing that "spiritually homeless, divorced from all custom and tradition, these white-collar workers sought refuge in entertainment – or the 'distraction industries.'"[18] The book provided a critical look at the lifestyle and culture of the new class of some "3.5 million" white-collar employees, or office workers, whose life, he wrote, is an "unknown territory." As a kind of "new middle class," their "existential insecurity increased," and "their prospect of independence has almost entirely disappeared." They differed from "the worker proletariat in that that *they are spiritually homeless*," belonging neither to the bourgeoisie or to the proletariat.[19] In cultural terms, Kracauer continually returns to the *Haus Vaterland* (Fatherland House) in Berlin, "an entertainment palace in which the culture of the office workers during the Weimar Republic thrived, as it did in the cinema palaces and department stores."[20] Three years later, many of these lower middle-class employees were quick to adopt Nazism and "flee into the arms of Adolph Hitler."[21]

In a contemporary review of *Die Angestellten*, Walter Benjamin praised the concreteness of Kracauer's analysis, which revealed that "[t]here is no

[18] Kracauer, quoted on the back cover without more specific attribution, *Salaried Masses*.

[19] Kracauer, *Salaried Masses*, 29–33, 88. A similar idea of the middle class as "spiritually homeless" appears in Erich Fromm's *Escape from Freedom* (New York: Rinehart & Company, 1941), 96, where he asserts that since the Protestant Reformation, the middle class has been "envious of those who had wealth and power and could enjoy life" and "rationalized this resentment and envy of life in terms of moral indignation and in the conviction that these superior people would be punished by eternal suffering."

[20] Koch, *Siegfried Kracauer*, 43.

[21] The quote is taken from the back cover of *Salaried Masses*.

class today whose thinking and feeling is more alienated from the concrete reality of its everyday existence than the salariat ... accommodation to the degradation and inhumane side of the present order has progressed further among salaried employees than among wage workers."[22] Later, in *From Caligari to Hitler*, Kracauer emphasized the inextricable connection between the middle class's shift from rebellion—the 1918 November Revolution that resulted in the replacement of the German federal constitutional monarchy with the democratic parliamentary republic that became known as the Weimar Republic—to submission to Nazism, as evidenced by the Weimar movies. He wrote: "the middle-class German's reluctance to emancipate himself originated in the fear of losing not only social privileges, but also those multifaceted potentialities he thought he had discovered within himself" (123).

As a member of Benjamin and Adorno's intellectual circles and sometimes associated with the Frankfurt School of Critical Theory, Kracauer became increasingly critical of capitalism and eventually left the *Frankfurter Zeitung*, although he was also very critical of Stalinism. At about the same time he married Lili Ehrenreich, a librarian at the Frankfurt University Institute for Social Research. After the Reichstag fire in February 1933, the couple escaped to Paris, and after the Nazis conquered France in 1940 they fled to the United States on April 15, 1941.[23] On the eve of their departure, Kracauer wrote to Adorno: "I will arrive" in America "a poor man, poorer than I have ever been," knowing perfectly well that at the age of fifty, "Now comes the last station, the last chance, which I must not gamble away, lest everything be lost."[24]

In 1937, Max Horkheimer, former director of the Institute of Social Research and now ensconced at Columbia University in New York, wrote to inform Kracauer that the city's Museum of Modern Art had an almost complete collection of German films and wished to conduct a study on the relationship between social development and cinema in Germany. Kracauer submitted a proposal, and two years later, in 1939, John Abbot, director of the New York Film Library, approved it and offered him a position. From 1941 to 1943, Kracauer worked in the film division of the Museum of Modern Art, supported by Guggenheim and Rockefeller Foundation

[22] Benjamin, "'An outsider attracts attention' – on *The Salaried Masses* by S. Kracauer," in Kracauer, *Salaried Masses*, 110.

[23] Moltke, *Curious Humanist*, 1.

[24] Ibid., 2.

grants.[25] In taking up this job, he must have felt he had been entrusted with a grand mission.

Six years later, *From Caligari to Hitler: A Psychological History of the German Film* (1947) appeared. Kracauer wrote it in English, another clear example of his unwavering *Kulturkampf* against Nazi barbarism—so as to appeal to a wider audience. The book is renowned, inter alia, for proposing a link between the apolitical and escapist orientation of Weimar-era cinema and the totalitarianism that followed. According to one biographer, given the context—the Nazi occupation of Europe and invasion of Russia—Kracauer erected "a veritable tower of books around himself in the library in order to better concentrate and seal himself off from other readers."[26] However, a recent study rejects this gloomy portrayal of Kracauer as a lone wolf; it argues convincingly that he "spent his American years networking, collaborating, and publishing."[27] Adorno observed that after Kracauer "managed to get [to America], he was in fact surprisingly successful."[28]

From Caligari to Hitler holds "that through an analysis of the German films, deep psychological dispositions predominant in Germany from 1918 to 1933 can be exposed – dispositions which influenced the course of events during that time and which *will have to be reckoned with in the post-Hitler era*" (li; emphasis added). Kracauer was well aware that the horrors of the Holocaust and other Nazi atrocities committed in World War II were multiplying. From the end of 1941 to the summer of 1942, news of the massacre of European Jews reached England and the United States.[29] In 1942 and 1943, Jan Karski (1914–2000), a Polish resistance fighter, reported to the Polish government in exile and the Western Allies on the destruction of the Warsaw ghetto and the secretive Nazi extermination camps.[30] These are the events Kracauer links to pre-Hitler German psychological dispositions with which we must now reckon.

[25] Quaresima, "Introduction," xix.

[26] Koch, *Siegfried Kracauer*, 76.

[27] Moltke, *Curious Humanist*, 10, 26–43.

[28] Ibid., 35.

[29] The ways in which early reports about the Holocaust reached Britain and the United States are discussed in Rafael Medoff, "How America First Learned of the Holocaust," *Jewish News Service*, 11 June 2012, http://www.jns.org/latest-articles/2012/6/11/how-america-first-learned-of-the-holocaust.html#.VTiUXPAauZE

[30] E. Thomas Wood and Stanisław M. Jankowski, *Karski: How One Man Tried to Stop the Holocaust* (Hoboken: John Wiley & Sons, 1994).

In 1960, Kracauer published *Theory of Film: The Redemption of Physical Reality*, in which he argues that realism is the most important function of cinema. Toward the end of his life, he worked as a sociologist at various institutions, including a spell as a director of research in the applied social sciences at Columbia University. He died in 1966; *History: The Last Things Before the Last* (1969) was published posthumously. Here, he revealed the existential trauma of his exilic displacement:

> I am thinking of the exile who as *an adult person has been forced to leave his country* or left it of his own ... Where then does he live? *In the near-vacuum of extra-territoriality, the very no-man's-land* ... The exile's true mode of existence is that of a stranger ... [In] *exile he is faced with the task – the exile's task – of penetrating its outward appearance, so that he may learn to understand that world from within.*[31]

From Caligari to Hitler should be read in light of this profound agony, which clearly spurred Kracauer to write it and recalls Adorno's remark that "the only home truly available" to exiles, "though fragile and vulnerable, is in writing."[32]

Finally, it is interesting to note that in *History,* Kracauer turned to Jewish themes, closely associating his exilic experience with that of the Wandering Jew, condemned to walk the earth until the Second Coming because he mocked Jesus along the way to the Crucifixion. Writing about "Ahasuerus, or the riddle of time," Kracauer argued that the chronicler is a survivor who has passed through the dark lens of time unscathed. He wrote: "the only real informant" about the course and progress of history

> is a legendary figure – Ahasuerus, the Wandering Jew. He indeed knows firsthand the developments and transactions, for he alone in all history has had the unsought opportunity to experience the process of becoming and decaying itself. (How unspeakably terrible he must look! To be sure, his face cannot have suffered from aging, but I imagine it to be many faces, each reflecting one of the periods which he traversed and all of them combining into ever new patterns, as he restlessly, and vainly, tries on his wandering to

[31] Kracauer, *History: The Last Things Before the Last* (Princeton: Princeton University Press, 1995), 83–84; emphasis added.

[32] Adorno, quoted in Edward Said, *Reflections on Exile and Other Essays* (Cambridge, MA: Harvard University Press, 2000), 184.

reconstruct out of the times that shaped him the one time he is doomed or incarnate.)[33]

In these bleak reflections, Kracauer is clearly writing about himself, a survivor whose great mission is "*to reconstruct out of the times that shaped him the one time he is doomed or incarnate*," or to chronicle the psychological history of the German film, which led to the Nazism that drove him out of Germany.

Other secular Jewish intellectuals exiled from Nazi Germany likewise took up Jewish subjects and themes. In *An Essay on Man* (1944), Cassirer offered a strong defense of Jewish thought and highly praised the Old Testament as one source of Western humanism, freedom, and the rise of the ethical standpoint in religious consciousness. Writing about "our own European civilization," he stressed that "the great prophets of Israel no longer spoke merely to their nations. Their God was a god of Justice and His message was not restricted to a special group." The ultimate message of this "prophetic religion" was "its ethical meaning."[34] In *Mimesis*, Auerbach constructed a grand *apologia* for the Old Testament's validity and credibility, revealing, through a dazzling analysis of literary works spanning three thousand years, that it is the foundation of Western culture and civilization as a whole, rather than the works of Homer, as maintained by Aryan philology and Nazi historiography.[35] Furthermore, one of the main arguments of Horkheimer and Adorno's *Dialectic of Enlightenment* is the contention that the overall humanization process, rejecting myth,

[33] Kracauer, *History*, 157. The German-Jewish writer Stefan Heym wrote a wonderful book on this theme—*Ahasver* (1981)—published in English as *The Wandering Jew* (1984). Ahasverus and Lucifer are both angels cast out of heaven for their views on God's order. The protest of Ahasverus is rooted in love and faith in progress, while Lucifer rebels through his old, familiar methods. In an amusing series of interminable run-ins, debates, and confrontations with characters such as Christ, a disciple of Luther, and a Marxist professor in East Germany, Ahasverus and Lucifer struggle onward, awaiting the Second Coming.

[34] Cassirer, *An Essay on Man: An Introduction to A Philosophy of Human Culture* (New Haven: Yale University Press, 1944), 103.

[35] On Erich Auerbach's turn to Jewish thought and culture, see Avihu Zakai, *Erich Auerbach and the Crisis of German Philology: The Humanist Tradition in Peril* (Dordrecht: Springer, 2017); *The Pen Confronts the Sword: Exiled German Scholars Challenge Nazism* (Albany: SUNY, 2018); and David Weinstein and Avihu Zakai, *Jewish Exiles and European Thought in the Shadow of the Third Reich: Baron, Popper, Strauss, Auerbach* (Cambridge: Cambridge University Press, 2017).

power, and domination in favor of rationalism, is inextricable from the "Jewish Question." They wrote:

> Only the *liberating of thought from power*, the abolition of violence, could realize the idea which has been unrealized until now: *that the Jew is a human being*. This would be a step away from the anti-Semitic society, which drives both Jews and others into sickness, and toward the human one. Such a step would fulfill the fascist lie by contradicting it: *the Jewish question would indeed prove the turning point of history.*[36]

Influences

> Any attempt to understand the attraction which Fascism exercises upon great nations compels us to recognize the role of psychological factors. For we are dealing here with a political system which, essentially, does not appeal to rational forces of self-interest, but which arouses and mobilizes diabolical forces in man ... (Fromm, *Escape from Freedom*, 1941 (7))

Nowadays, according to Leonardo Quaresima in his introduction to the revised and expanded 2004 edition of *From Caligari to Hitler*, its echo "is heard mainly in academic circles" (xviii). However, this fact should not hinder us from seeing it as an integral part of a well-defined *Kulturkampf* waged against Nazi and fascist totalitarianism by exiled intellectuals from Nazi Germany. The list of works is an impressive one and includes those written by Erich Fromm, Max Horkheimer, Theodore Adorno, Franz Leopold Neumann, Karl Popper, Ernst Cassirer, Erich Auerbach, Thomas Mann, Erich Neumann, Hannah Arendt, Leo Strauss, Hans Baron, and many others.[37] Their lot was the lost cause of humanism and freedom in Nazi Germany; hence, in exile, they all sharpened their intellectual tools to defeat its claim to *imperium sine fine* (rule without end).

In their strenuous confrontation with Nazi barbarism, these thinkers all engaged politics from their own particular disciplinary strength: Mann in literature, Fromm in psychology and sociology, Horkheimer and Adorno

[36] Horkheimer and Adorno, *Dialectic of Enlightenment,* 165; emphasis original. An analysis of the variety of Jewish subjects and themes addressed in these works can be found in Zakai, *Pen Confronts the Sword* and *Erich Auerbach.*

[37] An analysis of the content and form of some of these works that decried Nazi barbarism can be found in Zakai, *The Pen Confronts the Sword*; *Erich Auerbach and the Crisis of German Philology: The Humanist Tradition in Peril*; and, with David Weinstein, *Jewish Exiles and European Thought in the Shadow of the Third Reich.*

in philosophy and sociology, Franz Neumann in political science, Popper in philosophy, Cassirer in philosophy and political science, Auerbach in literary criticism and philology, Arendt in philosophy and political theory, Erich Neumann in psychology, Strauss in political philosophy, Baron in history, and Kracauer in films. Their constant point of reference was Nazism; they all analyzed and contested it with the liberty and perspective exile afforded. Thus, exile led to interpretation.

In deconstructing German history in the first half of the twentieth century through cinema, *From Caligari to Hitler* may be "the epitome of Germanness in its fatal conflation of art and politics."[38] The same overt intermingling of art and politics is evident in Mann's *Doctor Faustus*; chapter 34 describes a lengthy 1919 discussion on aestheticism as a precursor of barbarism and the re-barbarization of German culture as a precursor of Nazism. The debates address the decline of individualism and the old liberal bourgeois concepts of culture, Enlightenment, humanism, and progress. A prominent participant in the discussions is the nationalist, chauvinist, imperialist, and Fascist young poet Daniel Zur Höhe, who "loved to cross his arms over his chest or to hide one Napoleonic hand in his bosom," a clear reference to the posture of Adenoid Hynkel (Hitler) in Charlie Chaplin's film *The Great Dictator* (1940).[39] His "poetic dreams told of a world that bloody crusade had made subject to pure Spirit and that was kept in fear by the Spirit's sublime discipline." He produces only one poem, "Proclamations," which is "a lyrico-rhetorical outburst of voluptuous terrorism," supported by the signature of "an entity named Christus Imperator Maximus, an Energy who enlisted and commanded troops prepared to die in the cause of subjugation of the globe." Clearly, this poet is a forerunner of Nazism: "Proclamations" concludes with the cry, "Soldiers! I entrust to you the plundering – of the world,"[40] recalling John Dryden's 1697 translation of Virgil's *Aeneid*: "'tis thine alone, with

[38] Elsaesser, *Weimar Cinema*, 62.

[39] Chaplin was a friend of Mann, and they met frequently in the USA. "I have unlimited admiration for well-aimed parody," wrote Mann. "I greet Charlie Chaplin at a party." See Mann, *The Story of a Novel: The Genesis of Doctor Faustus*, trans. Richard Winston and Clara Winston (New York: Knopf, 1961), 207.

[40] Mann, *Doctor Faustus: The Life of the German Composer Adrian Leverkühn as Told by a Friend*, trans. John E. Wood (New York: Vintage, 1999), 383. For an analysis of this work, see Avihu Zakai, "Apocalypse and Eschatology in Thomas Mann's *Doctor Faustus*: The Secret Union of the German Spirit with the Demonic," in *Pen Confronts the Sword*, 23–82.

awful sway/To rule Mankind; and make the World obey," or the brief for the Nazi invasion of Czechoslovakia.[41]

Many other studies by exiles from Nazi Germany plumbed the "Age of Catastrophe"[42] or the "catastrophe of the fascist dictatorship."[43] No ivory tower scholars, these authors were all highly engaged in the politics of their time, waging a determined, strenuous, and meticulous *Kulturkampf* against the evil powers that had led to their traumatic forced exile. Among them, Kracauer is unique in pursuing answers in the popular media, and in his belief that movies are "cultural symbols in which the subjective characters that are developed function as markers for the collective identity."[44]

Kracauer's study should be examined in the light of two other works written by German-Jewish exiles that explored the psychological mechanisms that underpinned the "inherent weakness of the Social Democrats, the inadequate conduct of the communists and the strange reactions of the German masses" (10) that led to Hitler's rise and triumph. The first is Franz Neumann's *Behemoth: The Structure and Practice of National Socialism 1933–1944* (1944), which compares Nazi Germany to Behemoth, a monster from Jewish mythology, blindly worshiped by land animals.[45] His complex analysis shows that behind the autocratic façade of the Nazi regime lay nothing but the unbridled terror, egotism, and arbitrariness of certain social groups. Kracauer quoted Neumann, who explained the failure of the Weimar communists in terms of "their inability to evaluate

[41] See Hitler's speech at the NSDAP (National Socialist German Workers' Party) Congress in 1938: "I am asking neither that Germany be allowed to oppress three and a half million Frenchmen, nor am I asking that three and a half million Englishmen be placed at our mercy. Rather I am simply demanding that the oppression of three and a half million Germans in Czechoslovakia cease and that the inalienable right to self-determination take its place."

[42] Eric Hobsbawm. *The Age of Extremes: The Short Twentieth Century, 1914–1991* (New York: Pantheon, 1994), 6–7.

[43] Theodore W. Adorno, "The Curious Realist: On Siegfried Kracauer" (1964), in Adorno, *Notes to Literature*, ed. Rolf Tiedemann (New York: Columbia University Press, 1992), 2:73.

[44] Gertrud Koch, *Siegfried Kracauer: An Introduction* (Princeton: Princeton University Press, 2000), 80.

[45] In Jewish eschatology—of Babylonian origin—the male Behemoth rules the land (the desert), and the female Leviathan, the sea. Land animals venerate Behemoth; sea animals revere Leviathan. The two monsters are due to reappear shortly before the end of the world and establish a rule of terror, but God will destroy them.

correctly the psychological factors" operating "among the German workers" (10; emphasis added).[46]

The second was *Escape from Freedom*. Kracauer admitted that his construction of psychological history owed a great deal to "the social psychology of Erich Fromm."[47] At approximately the same time that Kracauer was working on *The Salaried Masses*, Fromm was collaborating with three colleagues on "The Character of German Workers and Employees in 1929/30," a sociological study of the appeal of Nazi ideology to the lower middle class. According to Kracauer, Fromm showed that "German workers' psychological tendencies neutralized their political tenets, thus precipitating the collapse of the socialist parties and the trade-unions" (10–11).

In exile, Kracauer and Fromm both wrote comprehensive historical, sociological, and psychological interpretations of the rise and success of Nazism. Their traumatic displacement led to conduct an exhaustive, atavistic search for the factors that had destroyed their beloved homeland and driven them from it. Fromm analyzed the psychologically slippery notion of freedom in Western history, and Kracauer explored the psychology of such classic German films as *The Cabinet of Dr. Caligari* (1920) and *Metropolis* (1927) as harbingers of fascism. (Neither of them seems to have examined his snooty generalizations about "other" people or compared them to Nazi generalizations about, say, the Jews).

From Caligari to Hitler was written in the midst of World War II. It was commissioned within a specific, concrete, clear-cut ideological and historical framework of the war against Nazism—to determine the influence of German films on social development and the rise and triumph of Nazism. Obviously, just as much as his sponsors in the United States, Kracauer was eager to know the enemy in order to fight and defeat it. The same pressing goal inspired Fromm's highly combative *Escape from Freedom*, written in response to the "[p]resent political developments and the dangers which they imply for the greatest achievements of modern culture—individuality and the uniqueness of personality." Fromm held that "*If we want to fight Fascism we must understand it*."[48]

[46] See Neumann, *Behemoth: The Structure and Practice of National Socialism 1933–1944* (1944; New York: Harper Torchbook, 1966), 18–19.

[47] Quaresima, "Introduction," xxix. On Fromm's book, see Zakai, "A Psychological Inquiry into Totalitarianism: Erich Fromm's *Escape from Freedom*," *Society*, 55, 5 (Fall 2018): 440–50

[48] Fromm, *Escape from Freedom*, vii, 5; emphasis added.

Kracauer shared this belief and objective, but his study also offers us his original and idiosyncratic observations on popular culture. According to Adorno, Kracauer believed "that when a medium desired and consumed by the masses transmits an ideology that is internally consistent and cohesive, this ideology is presumably adapting to the needs of the consumers as much as, conversely, it is progressively shaping them."[49] History influenced films as much as they influenced its course and progress. Kracauer's "psychologically key and teleological or 'retroactive' approach are oriented in a specific context."[50] He does not address trivial plots and petty aesthetic concerns but explores their relationship to the mass psychology of the period. Kracauer clarified: "The book is not concerned with German films merely for their own sake; rather, *it aims at increasing our knowledge of pre-Hitler Germany in a specific way*" (li; emphasis added). Underlying his approach is a teleological, deterministic view of history and the belief that psychology is the best means to track the Nazi flight from reason, freedom, democracy, and humanism.

Cultural Context

During the Weimar Republic and increasingly after the triumph of National Socialism in 1933, Germans felt they were "involved in a permanent crisis of nationhood and ideology" and saw themselves "as knights riding bravely between death and the devil," recalling Albrecht Dürer's woodcut *Knight, Death and the Devil* (1513). Not only in Germany but all over Europe, fascism "exhibited a flight from reality into the realm of emotional and mystical ideology." Fascist movements "were all part of the 'displaced revolution' which moved *from a rejection of reality to glorification of ideology*."[51] Kracauer aims to reveal the gathering clouds, "exposing the German soul" (3) through its cinematic expression.

He believed that "films of a nation reflect its mentality in a more direct way than other artistic media" (5). They reveal "not so much explicit credos as psychological dispositions – those deep layers of collective mentality which extend more or less below the dimension of consciousness." As

[49] Adorno, "Curious Realist," 66.

[50] Quaresima, "Introduction," xxxviii.

[51] George L. Mosse, *The Crisis of German Ideology: Intellectual Origins of the Third Reich* (New York: Grosset & Dunlap, 1964), 203; emphasis added. On the demonic strain in Dürer's works, see Andrew Butterfield, "Dürer's Devil Within," at http://www.nybooks.com/blogs/nyrblog/2013/may/20/durer-devil-within/

such, movies "mirror" or "record" the "visible world – whether current reality or an imaginary universe." They also "provide clues to hidden mental processes," which have a national or a cultural background: "the unseen dynamics of human relations are more or less characteristic of the inner life of the nation from which the films emerge" (7). Constantly aware of the present catastrophe, Kracauer contended that defining these "psychological dispositions" through the medium of the German screen "*may help in the understanding of Hitler's ascent and ascendancy*" (11; emphasis added).

Nazi ideology and historiography were based on *völkisch* mysticism, racism, chauvinism, and the mythologies of blood and soil (*Blut und Boden*), or the Community of Blood and Fate of the German people, glorifying the concept of a strictly German *Kultur* and rejecting the concept of European humanist civilization. Thomas Mann had no illusions about Nazi Germany; in 1940, he wrote:

> Where there is Nazism, there is to be found the denial of every decent human attribute and a reversion to the pagan and barbaric state of life in which murder, corruption, and intrigue are not merely condoned but advocated. Truth, justice, dignity have been ideals cherished by free men through the ages, but under Hitlerism they are simply empty words.[52]

In speaking about the peculiar mentality of German film, Kracauer was not conceding a *Kultur*; his approach by no means implied "the concept of a fixed national character" elevated above time and history. As a historicist, his interest lay rather in the "collective dispositions or tendencies" that were "preserved within a nation at a certain stage of its development"; for example, what "fears and hopes swept Germany immediately after World War I?" Such specific questions, he argued, "are the only ones which can be answered by an appropriate analysis of the films of that time" (8). The emphasis on fears and hopes explains why psychology is crucial to any possible understanding of the course of modern history in general and modern German history in particular.

Kracauer's sense of history may be seen as a direct—and an ironic—response to Germany's "special path." World War I and the 1919 Treaty of Versailles "imposed new strictures upon German historical scholarship and led to a new retreat to a nationalist position." German historians of

[52] Mann to Edward Edwards, June 23, 1940, in *Letters of Thomas Mann, 1889–1955*, sel. and trans. Richard Winston and Clara Winston (New York: Knopf, 1971), 340.

the 1920s saw their main task as justifying "the country's historical path since Bismarck, the rejection of Germany's war guilt – in short a defense of Germany's 'special path'" in history, or "the *Sonderweg*."[53] The 1920s also witnessed "the völkisch revolution" in German history and historiography, which "became an anti-Jewish revolution." Of course, nationalist ideology existed well before the Great War, "but afterward it was suddenly transformed into a politically effective system of thought." It was only "after the war that the ideology acquired a mass base."[54] The change was evident among professional historians: "The *völkisch* forces rapidly increased their influence among the younger nationalists during the 1920s."[55] The Babel of Hitlerism arose in the Weimar Republic.

Kracauer's ultimate goal is to enhance "our knowledge of pre-Hitler Germany" (li) through the medium best suited *to show* "the psychological pattern of a people at a particular time." Since there was "no lack of studies covering the political, social, economic and cultural history of the great nations," he proposed to add the important dimension of "*psychological history*" (8; emphasis added). At the same time, he blended the psychological and the sociological perspectives, which he deemed inseparable. Like Fromm in *Escape from Freedom* and Horkheimer and Adorno in *Dialectic of Enlightenment*, he emphasized the crucial historical role of a specific social class—the middle class, or the bourgeoisie—at major turning points, such as the 1918 and 1933 revolutions, and in the Weimar Republic. Fromm wrote that "moral indignation ... has invariably been *characteristic of the lower middle class from Luther's time to Hitler's.*"[56] Horkheimer and Adorno argued that with "the spread of bourgeois commodity economy the dark horizon of myth is illuminated by the sun of calculating reason, beneath whose icy rays the seeds of *the new barbarism* are germinating."[57] In the same vein, Kracauer asserted that in "pre-Nazi Germany, middle-class penchants penetrated all strata; they competed

[53] Ernst Schulin, "German and American Historiography in the Nineteenth and Twentieth Centuries," in *Interrupted Past: German-Speaking Refugee Historians in the United States after 1933*, ed. Hartmut Lehmann and James J. Sheehan (Cambridge, UK: Cambridge University Press, 1991), 19.

[54] Mosse, *Crisis of German Ideology: Intellectual Origins of the Third Reich* (1964; New York: Howard Fertig, 1998), v, 237, 243.

[55] Fritz K. Ringer, *The Decline of the German Mandarins: The German Academic Community, 1890–1933* (Cambridge, MA: Harvard University Press, 1969), 436.

[56] Fromm, *Escape from Freedom*, 96; emphasis added.

[57] Horkheimer and Adorno, *Dialectic of Enlightenment*, 25.

with the political aspirations of the Left and also filled the voids of the upper-class mind." This sociological perspective accounts for "the nation-wide appeal of the cinema – *a cinema firmly rooted in middle class mentality*" (8; emphasis added). Bourgeois psychology, according to these firmly bourgeois Jewish exiles from Nazi Germany, was responsible to a large extent for Hitler's ascent and facilitated the Nazi revolution.

Kracauer used the method of *Geistesgeschichte*, or intellectual history, to speak about "the soul of a people," the "German mind," and the "collective soul," but he was always referring to a specific group—the middle class. Like Fromm, he read contemporary German history almost exclusively in terms of the middle class, and in this context, *From Caligari to Hitler* can be seen as a direct continuation of *The Salaried Masses*, which also offers "an anticipatory diagnosis of the contradictions, distortions and delusions that the National Socialists were to mobilize a few years later."[58] Both studies posit a disconnection between the material conditions of the middle class and the forms by which it represented itself. While "the position of these strata in the economic process has changed; their middle-class conception of life has remained."[59] In economic terms, the German middle class during the 1920s was in decline, and its material conditions "resembled those of the working class."[60] It became to a great extent "proletarianized," in Kracauer's words: "they are homeless"; the "house of bourgeois ideas and feelings in which they used to live has collapsed, its foundations eroded by economic development."[61] In psychological terms, salaried employees' social and economic plight led to alienation and resentment. According to Fromm, the entire human condition was profoundly transformed: "Man was deprived of security he had enjoyed, of the unquestionable feeling of belonging, and he was torn loose from the world which had satisfied his quest for security both economically and spiritually. He felt alone and anxious."[62]

In a review of *The Salaried Masses*, Walter Benjamin vividly captured the way in which their ongoing economic decline led the middle class to flee everyday life: "Reality is so greatly neglected that it must show its colours and name names."[63] Kracauer quoted a contemporary, who was asked why

[58] Inka Mülder-Bach, "Introduction," *Salaried Masses*, 5–6.
[59] Kracauer, *Salaried Masses*, 81.
[60] Ibid., 5–6.
[61] Ibid., 88.
[62] Ibid., 99.
[63] Benjamin, "'An outsider attracts attention' – on *The Salaried Mass* by S. Kracauer," 109.

people spent so much time in bars: "Probably because things are so miserable at home and they want to get a bit of glamour." Benjamin was quick to point out that "home" should be taken "to mean not just lodging but an everyday existence."[64] Kracauer adopted the same socio-psychological examination of individual features of middle-class social life, such as sports and bar-hopping, to explore film in *From Caligari to Hitler*.

According to Kracauer, during the Golden Era of the Weimar Republic, as the economy grew and, consequently, civil unrest subsided, "paralysis of mind [was] spreading throughout Germany." With the Great Depression of 1929, the "collective paralysis" merely worsened; "psychological tendencies often assume independent life" and become "essential springs of historical evolution." In a time of great crisis and "extreme political change," collective dispositions gained momentum. The "dissolution of political systems results in the decomposition of psychological systems, and in the ensuing turmoil traditional inner attitudes, now released, are bound to become conspicuous, whether they are challenged or endorsed" (9). Traditional interpretations could not capture the magnitude of the crisis; they were insufficient "to explain the tremendous impact of Hitlerism and the chronic inertia in the opposing camp." (9).

In *The Salaried Masses*, Kracauer had argued that "lower middle-class people could no longer hope for bourgeois security" and, hence, "scorned all doctrines and ideals more in harmony with their plight, maintaining attitudes that had lost any basis in reality." Now in America, adopting Fromm's views on the middle-class's sense of isolation, he contended that their loss of any real advantages over the working class resulted in "mental forlornness: they persisted in a kind of vacuum which added further to their psychological obduracy."

> The conduct of the petty bourgeoisie proper was particularly striking. Small shopkeepers, tradesmen and artisans were so full of resentments that they shrank from adjusting themselves. Instead of realizing that it might be in their practical interest to side with democracy, they preferred, like the employees, to listen to Nazi promises. Their surrender to the Nazis was based on *emotional fixations* rather than on any facing of facts. (11; emphasis added)

[64] Ibid., 88.

Kracauer concludes that "[b]ehind the overt history of economic shifts, social exigencies and political machinations runs a secret history involving the inner dispositions of the German people. The disclosure of these through the medium of the German screen may help in the understanding of Hitler's ascent and ascendancy" (11).

In simple historical terms, Kracauer believes that German history runs a coherent, inevitable course from devastating defeat in World War I to the terrible demise of democracy under Hitler, a process that can be analyzed by viewing the German films of the period as omens. An apocalyptic and eschatological history based on revelation and judgment is at work here, although it is focused:

> This book is not concerned with establishing some national character pattern allegedly elevated above history, but is concerned with the psychological pattern of a people at a particular time. There is no lack of studies covering the political, social, economic and cultural history of the great nations. I proposed to add to these well-known types that of psychological history. (p. 8)

Cinema assumes the role of primary source material. It not only adapted to its consumers' needs but shaped them along with their persuasions, reasoning, and modes of conduct. Films determined the psychological conditions of their mass audience; as a result, Nazi Germany "*carried out what has been anticipated by her cinema*" (272; emphasis added). Social, economic, and political factors shaped the existential and psychological conditions of the middle class in particular and German history in general during the Weimar Republic, but the culture industry contributed enormously to the transformation of people's consciousness. Kracauer's book is a psychological history, not only of the German film but of the Weimar Republic itself, viewed "through a glass, darkly."[65]

From Caligari to Hitler: *Kulturkampf*, Apocalypse, and Eschatology

> The films of a nation reflect its mentality in a more direct way than other artistic media. (Kracauer, *From Caligari to Hitler* (5))

[65] 1 Corinthians 13, verse 12: "For now we see through a glass, darkly; but then face to face: now I know in part; but then shall I know even as also I am known."

> [A] premier film critic ... is only conceivable as a social critic .... His mission is to uncover the social ideas and ideologies concealed in your average film. (Kracauer, *From Caligari to Hitler* (75))

Why did Kracauer choose *Caligari* for the title of his book? It is not the first film he discusses. He did so because although legions of fictional characters walk the stage of the Weimar films, it was *The Cabinet of Dr. Caligari* that inspired of them. Furthermore, a book's title reveals intention and meaning. Change it, and you wrest it from the history that bore it; you drift away from the author's understanding of its content and form. Like the tiles of many other books written by exiles from Nazi Germany, Kracauer's reflects, directly or indirectly, the trauma of his rude separation from his beloved mother culture when it betrayed him and turned toward myth and unreason. In literature, Thomas Mann's *Doctor Faustus* renders Nazi Germany as the new incarnation of the old German legend of amoral arrogance and ambition; it equates Germany's covenant with Nazism with a contract with the devil and predicts the same apocalyptic destruction. In political philosophy, Ernst Cassirer's *The Myth of the State* denounced *Blut und Boden*, the toxic mythology that led to the systematic extermination of people deemed alien and the rapacious seizure of land deemed *Heimat* (home). Cassirer also condemned philosophers, such as Oswald Spengler (1880-1936) and Martin Heidegger (1889-1976), for supporting the German culture of pessimism, fatalism, and paranoia, or the destructive "myth of the state." In philology, Auerbach's *Mimesis* contested the Nazi rejection of the Old Testament and Jewish influence on European humanist civilization, taking up the ancient Greek debate about the relative value of mythic versus mimetic art to elevate ordinary human dignity above specious superheroes. Finally, in sociology, Horkheimer and Adorno's *Dialectic of Enlightenment* illuminated how Enlightenment rhetoric was driven by a myth of power, first over nature, then over other people, and led to the subjugation – indeed, destruction – of the powerless by the powerful.[66]

Films not only reflect the inner, psychological life of a nation but shape and direct it. Psychological tendencies often assume an independent life, Kracauer believed, and became "essential springs of historical evolution" (9). The title of his book reveals the intertwining of movies and history in his thought: from *an* incarnation of evil to *the* incarnation of evil. The popularity of movies' "pictorial and narrative motifs" and their "persistent

[66] For an analysis of these works, see Zakai *Pen Confronts the Sword.*

reiteration" mark them "as outward projections of inner urges." Thus, the history of "the German screen is a history of motifs pervading films" (8). Film for Kracauer is an "epistemic screen onto which national introspection is projected."[67] History, psychology, and ideology intermingle in the German cinema. Kracauer begins with a film about a hypnotist and postulates that film *is* the hypnotist, and the audience the somnambulistic victim.

Kracauer read German history as moving inexorably *From Caligari to Hitler*; the terror of Hitler's politics was the realistic fulfillment of the terrors of the silent movie about the crazed hypnotist Dr. Caligari. He believed that since Germany "carried out what has been *anticipated by her cinema*," conspicuous "screen characters now came true in life itself." In this "unholy procession, *many motifs known from the screen turned into actual events*" (272; emphasis added). Satanic, insane characters were not merely artistic performances but prefigured people who would play real roles in history. Films not only reveal the psychological dispositions of a nation but also foretell actual events. Kracauer's teleological, apocalyptic, eschatological, and deterministic view of history reads movies as prescient. His interpretation of German history is figural; that is, events and characters in the German movies are *figures* or *prefigurations* of real-world events and persons.

Many consider *The Cabinet of Dr. Caligari* (*Das Cabinet des Dr. Caligari*, 1920) the first true horror film and the quintessential work of German expressionist cinema. Lotte H. Eisner (1896–1983) wrote that with this movie, "the German cinema found its true nature."[68] Historians of Weimar culture Peter Gay and Walter Laqueur asserted that this movie, among other works of art, "defined its Zeitgeist."[69] It exercised enormous influence on many contemporary genres: tyrant movies, destiny movies, and instinct movies. By contrast to Mann's *Doctor Faustus*, which was based on a fifteenth-century German legend, the script of *The Cabinet of Dr. Caligari* was written by Hans Janowitz and Carl Mayer, both pacifists, who were left distrustful of authority after their military experiences during World War I. It tells the story of an insane hypnotist who uses a sleepwalking surrogate to commit murders. Kracauer contended that the film

[67] Ibid., 81.

[68] Lotte Eisner, *The Haunted Screen: Expressionism in the German Cinema and the Influence of Max Reinhardt* (Berkeley and Los Angeles: University of California Press, 1969), 17.

[69] Elsaesser, *Weimar Cinema*, 61.

presents surrender to Caligari's tyranny as the only alternative to the socially chaotic fairground. He cites the name of the movie in the title of his book to highlight it as an allegory of German social and psychological attitudes in the period following World War I. More generally, Weimar films, such as *The Golem* (1915), *The Cabinet of Dr. Caligari* (1920), *Dr. Mabuse, the Gambler* (1922), and *Metropolis* (1927), were forerunners of Nazism, reflecting the murky alliance of cinema and politics.

Kracauer picks out *Caligari* because it "exerted such a hypnotic as well as hermeneutic fascination on the critics of the day and continued to do so for every generation since."[70] For him, "*Caligari* exposes the soul wavering between tyranny and chaos, and facing a desperate situation: any escape from tyranny seems to throw it into a state of utter confusion. Quite logically, the film spreads an all-pervading atmosphere or horror. *Like the Nazi world, that of* Caligari *overflows with sinister portent, acts of terror and outbursts of panic*" (74; emphasis added). Caligari is the harbinger of doom of the Weimar Republic.

The Cabinet of Dr. Caligari embodies the apocalyptic and eschatological dimension throughout. Caligari's power is symptomatic of German society's subconscious need for a tyrant. As a premonition of Hitler, his control over the weak-willed, puppet-like somnambulist Cesare also prefigures the mentality of those who followed the Nazi Party. Caligari "uses his hypnotic power to force his will upon his tool – *a technique foreshadowing, in content and purpose, that manipulation of the soul which Hitler was the first to practice on a gigantic scale*" (72–73; emphasis added). Through cinema, Caligari's reach is multiplied and magnified. Adorno took note of the same paralyzing spell of Nazism, or "paralysis of mind" (9). In June 1940, after the Nazi invasion of France, he wrote to his parents: "We are trying at least to keep a cool head and not be numbed by horror. But this horror has meanwhile taken on such proportions that even that is no easy matter, *one falls into a sort of frozen state, like the bird staring at the snake.*"[71]

The film enacts Germany's obedience to authority and failure or unwillingness to rebel against deranged authority, reflected in the "general retreat" into "a shell" after the war (75, 120). Cesare's mindlessness foreshadows a German future in which "self-appointed Caligaris hypnotized innumerable Cesares into murder" (272). Thomas Mann employed the

[70] Ibid., 62.

[71] June 11, 1940, in Adorno, *Letters to his Parents: 1939–1951* (Cambridge, UK: Polity, 2006), 56; emphasis added.

same theme in *Mario and the Magician* (1929), where the hypnotist magician Cavalier Cipolla, like the Fascist dictators of the era, controls audiences with fiery speeches and rhetoric; he is a "dreadful being" who seems to represent "all the peculiar evilness" of the time, and Mario is viewed as a hero for murdering him.[72] Cassirer, Horkheimer, and Adorno all shared the view that Nazi rabble-rousing was a form of ancient hypnotism. Cassirer compared it to the beautiful witch-goddess Circe who turned Odysseus's men into pigs,[73] and Horkheimer and Adorno drew similar parallels with the Sirens,[74] the beautiful yet dangerous *femmes fatales*, whose enchanting voices lured sailors to shipwreck on the rocky coast of their island.[75]

From Caligari to Hitler makes an important claim: as popular art, films provide insights into the unconscious motivations and fantasies of a nation. In the films of the 1920s, Kracauer traced recurring visual and narrative tropes that expressed, so he argued, a fear of chaos and desire for order, even at the price of authoritarian rule, which portended the Nazi revolution of 1933. The cinema became a reliable and crucial source of insight into historical change. Kracauer's book has become a classic of film historiography, laying the foundations for the serious study of film.

The book identifies four distinct periods: the Archaic Period (1895–1918); the Postwar Period (1918–1924), characterized by "*monologue intérieur*" (60) and flight from reason and reality; the Stabilized Period (1924–1929), or a state of paralysis, when films reveal that "the desperate struggle for psychological adjustment was a general strengthening of the authoritarian tendencies" (137); and finally, the pre-Hitler Period (1930–1933), in which previous attempts to maintain "neutrality for the sake of *status quo*" crumbled (211); "paralysis had subsided, and all kind of authoritarian leanings were manifested" (215). In the second and fourth periods, the German screen became a battleground of conflicting inner tendencies. The book also includes a reprint of a pamphlet released by the Museum of Modern Art in 1942, "Propaganda and the Nazi War Film." This critical and psychological analysis clearly reveals Kracauer's confrontational *Kulturkampf* against Nazism and Hitlerism.

[72] Thomas Mann, *Mario and the Magician* (New York: Knopf, 1931), 3.
[73] Cassirer, *Myth of the State*, 286.
[74] Horkheimer and Adorno, *Dialectic of Enlightenment*, 25–28.
[75] See Zakai, *The Pen Confronts the Sword.*

Kracauer was a well-known film critic in Germany and saw many of the films he discussed when they were first released; he was also well acquainted with movie directors, actors, and screenwriters; for example, Fritz Lang, Robert Wiene, and Hans Janowitz (61–67). He read German national cinema for its underlying sociopolitical and psychological meaning, viewing film as a medium of cultural expression. Perhaps he shared the view of Bruno Latour: "we are always prisoners of language."[76]

In *From Caligari to Hitler*, Kracauer aimed to define "the subterranean content that, like contraband, had crossed the borders of consciousness without being questioned" (31). In a letter to the poet and novelist Herman Hesse (1877–1962), he explained that the medium of films gave him "precise indications about the psychological disposition of the Germans."[77] He would use the psychoanalytic approach to discover "the connection between psychic process and cinema's technical and linguistic aspects."[78] He speaks of films as "reflecting" and "mirroring" (30) social and political reality. Hence, every "thematic linguistic component, every choice in the staging of a film discloses its meaning by referring to historical and social events"; for example, "every aspect of the rich cinematic history of the Weimar republic is precisely and persuasively corroborated"[79] as patterns and precedents realized in "Hitler's ultimate triumph" (9).

The Archaic Period, 1895–1918

"The German cinema really came into being," Kracauer wrote, only after the First World War; the period between 1895 and 1918 marks its "prehistory." Up until 1910, Germany had virtually no film industry, but "films of French, Italian and American origins" poured in. Between 1906 and 1908, "German films increased in length," which led to "the opening of many new theaters" (15). Ironically, World War I "freed the native industry from the burden of foreign competition," while increasing the demand for movies enormously: the number of German movie companies rose from 28 in 1913 to 245 in 1919. In other words, the German film

[76] Latour, "Why Has Critique Run Out of Steam? From Matters of Fact to Matters of Concern," *Critical Inquiry*, 30 (Winter 2004): 227.

[77] Kracauer quoted by Quaresima, "Introduction," xxxi.

[78] Ibid.

[79] Ibid., xxxii.

industry became "autonomous," and no longer "needed to emulate foreign products" (22).

Kracauer notes an immediate national distinction: while "the amiable French artist enchanted all childlike souls with his bright conjuring tricks, *the German actor proved a sinister magician calling up the demonian forces* of human nature" (28; emphasis added). From their inception, German films were possessed by the devil.

Clear support for this assertion can be found in the movie *The Student of Prague* (1913), which borrowed from E. T. A. Hoffmann, the Faust legend, and Edgar Allen Poe. A poor student, Baldwin, signs "a compact with the queer sorcerer Scapinelli," the "incarnation of Satan," who promises him "advantageous marriage and inexhaustible wealth" (29). Germans evidently tended to equate the devil with Italy, probably as a vestige of the Protestant Reformation. In 1545, a year before his death, Luther wrote *Against the Papacy at Rome, Founded by the Devil.* In it he claims that the Pope is a child of the devil, who seeks to destroy the Church through the lies of the Pope and the sword of the Turks. Caligari and Cesare are both Italian names. In *Mario and the Magician*, Mann's diabolical sorcerer and controller-of-wills Cavalier Cipolla is Italian. He delivers fiery speeches and rhetoric like the fascist dictators of the era; he is a "dreadful being" who seems to represent "all the peculiar evilness" of the time.[80] However, later, in *Doctor Faustus*, Mann switches the devil's sphere of action and center of influence to Germany, and the composer Adrian Leverkühn, the protagonist of this novel, is deeply astonished when the devil appears to him in the birthplace of Renaissance civic-humanism. He exclaims with great irony, "In Wittenberg or on the Wartburg, even in Leipzig I would have thought you credible," but "in Italy of all places, where you are quite out of your realm and enjoy not the least popularity? What an absurd want of fashion." The devil replies without the slightest hesitation: "German I shall be" and "German I am, German to the core." He enjoys "foremost German popularity," noting that "this world wherein we are together" presents "[g]ood times, devilish German times."[81] Nazism made Satan a native son, not a tourist.

[80] Mann, *Mario*, 3.

[81] Mann, *Doctor Faustus*, 242, 247.

The Postwar Period, 1918–1924

The shock of their devastating defeat in World War I and the enormous burden of the reparations levied on Germany by the 1919 Treaty of Versailles left an indelible mark on the German people and the German film: "Millions of Germans, in particular middle-class Germans, seem to have shut themselves off from a world determined by the Allied pressure, violent internal struggles and inflation." They acted as though under the influence of "a terrible shock which upset normal relations between their outer and inner existence" (59). In the early sixteenth century, Luther pointed to a deep, inherent chasm in the Christian soul: "A Christian man is the most free lord of all, and subject to none; a Christian man is the most dutiful servant of all, and subject to everyone."[82] Now, Kracauer emphasized this essential, latent dualism, claiming that in the wake of the First World War, Germans made a "psychological exodus from the outer world" (59). This unique atavism had serious consequences for the cinema of that time: "The films of the postwar period from 1920 to 1924 are a unique *monologue intérieur*. They reveal developments in almost inaccessible layers of the German mind" (60). First and foremost among them was *The Cabinet of Dr. Caligari*, the "archetype of all forthcoming post war film" (3).

Dr. Caligari, "a weird, bespectacled man advertising the somnambulist Cesare," has come to a fair in the fictitious north German town of Holstenwall (63)—in reality, a part of Hamburg. Most of the time, Cesare is kept in a box, his master's "cabinet," but during the performance Caligari invites the audience to hear Cesare foretell their future. The joyful fair is transformed at once into an awful site of terrible omens. Dr. Caligari opens the coffin-like box to reveal the sleeping Cesare, who, on Caligari's command, awakens and answers questions from the audience. Despite the protest of his friend Francis, Alan asks, "How long will I live?" and to his horror, Cesare answers, "Until dawn." Later that night, a figure breaks into Alan's home and stabs him to death in his bed. Grief-stricken, Francis resolves to investigate the murder.

Every scene in *The Cabinet of Dr. Caligari* "radiates horror and foreboding."[83] This psychological and criminal thriller, wrote Kracauer,

[82] See Luther, "On Christian Freedom" (1520); trans. H. Wace and C.A. Buckheim, in *First Principles of the Reformation* (Philadelphia, 1885); http://www-personal.k-state.edu/~lyman/english233/Luther-CF.htm/.

[83] Brockmann, *Critical History*, 64.

reflected "the tortured soul of contemporary Germany."[84] When finally caught by young Francis, Caligari flees to a lunatic asylum. Francis follows him and calls on the asylum's director to inquire about the fugitive. He "recoils, horror struck: the director and Caligari are one and the same person" (64).

Caligari's character, argued Kracauer, embodies profound, fatal tendencies latent in the German system (although he has an Italian name, as does Cesare): "he stands for an unlimited authority that idolizes power as such, and, to satisfy its lust for domination, ruthlessly violates all human rights and values." At the end of the film, with the disclosure that the asylum director is Caligari, "reason overpowers unreasonable power, insane authority is symbolically abolished" (65). If, during the postwar years, "most Germans eagerly tended to withdraw from a harsh outer world into the intangible realm of the soul," then the movie "faithfully mirrored the general retreat into a shell" (67). It is "an outward projection of psychological events"; the "expressionist staging" replaced the common sign "Men at Work" with "Soul at Work" (71).

Apart from analyzing the movie in psychological terms, Kracauer read the protagonist's hypnotic power, or manipulation of souls, politically. "Caligari is a very specific premonition in the sense that he uses his hypnotic power to force his will upon his tool – *a technique foreshadowing, in content and purpose, that manipulation of the soul which Hitler was the first to practice on a gigantic scale*" (72–73; emphasis added). It was this psychological, hypnotic dimension, argued Kracauer, that made the film so popular in Germany: Caligari is the prefiguration of Hitler and "[l]*ike the Nazi world, that of* Caligari *overflows with sinister portents, acts of terror and outbursts of panic*" (74; emphasis added).

The Holstenwall fair, the social space where Caligari first reveals his hypnotic, satanic powers, symbolizes this world. Traditionally, Kracauer explains, the fair was regarded as "an enclave of anarchy in the sphere of entertainment." It resembled "Babel and Babylon alike." An adult was permitted "a regression into childhood days," he "escapes a civilization which tends to overgrow and starve out the chaos of instincts – escapes it to restore that chaos upon which civilization nevertheless rests." At the fair, mental breakdown and insanity prevail. The connection to Weimar Germany is patently clear: *"The fair is not freedom, but anarchy entailing*

[84] Eisner, *Haunted Screen*, 17.

chaos" and "faithfully reflected the chaotic condition of postwar Germany" (73–74; emphasis added).

In both the film and real life, the "normal" is "a madhouse." Both "unleashed a strong *sadism and an appetite for destruction*"; enactment "of these traits on the screen *once more testifies to their prominence in the German collective soul*" (74; emphasis added). Kracauer sees the film's nightmare universe as the rule in the Nazi totalitarian regime.

In 1926, six years after *Caligari's* premiere, Hans Janowitz, who wrote the screenplay with Carl Meyer, traveled to Paris and called on the art patron Count Étienne de Beaumont (1883–1956). The count voiced his admiration for the movie, finding it "as fascinating and abstruse as *the German soul*." He declared that "the time has come for the German soul to speak," adding that the "French soul spoke more than a century ago, in the Revolution, and you have been mute." Now, he pleaded with Janowitz, "we are waiting for what you [the Germans] have to impart to us, to the world." Kracauer comments dryly: "The Count did not have long to wait" (76). The English had their Glorious Revolution at the end of the seventeenth century, and the Americans and French revolted against monarchy at the end of the eighteenth century. Perhaps the count expected a democratic revolution to erupt in the German soul and behavior. Instead, he and the entire world witnessed the Nazi return to barbarism, or by Kracauer's reasoning, the Caligari Revolution, the realization of Caligari, which ensured the triumph of Hitlerism, enslavement, and murder.

The Cabinet of Dr. Caligari exercised enormous influence on German films during the early 1920s. Its "basic theme – the soul being faced with the seemingly *unavoidable alternative of tyranny or chaos* – exerted extraordinary fascination" (77; emphasis added). A "shock of freedom" (43) followed the First World War, when a civil uprising replaced the constitutional monarchy with the Weimar Republic. *The Cabinet of Dr. Caligari* is among several movies produced at that time that "specialized in depicting of tyrants." They reflected "a people still unbalanced, still free to choose its regime," while detailing tyranny "and the suffering it inflicted." Kracauer remarks somewhat disingenuously: "It is, at any rate, a strange coincidence that, hardly more than a decade later, Nazi Germany was to put into practice that very mixture of physical and mental tortures which the German screen then pictured" (77). Hardly a "strange coincidence," given his overarching thesis that German films represent the German mind and soul on the path to the Nazi revolution.

Among the other movies symbolizing the "Processing of Tyrants" (77), Kracauer mentions the silent horror film *Nosferatu: A Symphony of Horror* (1922), an unauthorized adaptation of Bram Stoker's novel *Dracula* (1897), and another 1922 movie, *Vanina*, based on Stendhal's short story "Vanina Vanini" (1829), which focused on "the psychological causes and effects of tyranny."

A third important 1922 tyrant movie was Fritz Lang's *Dr. Mabuse, The Gambler*. This silent film, based on the pulp novel by Norbert Jacques, follows the devious schemes of a criminal mastermind. Like Dr. Caligari, Dr. Mabuse hypnotizes his victims and "evades identification by impersonating diverse characters" (81). Eventually, like Caligari, he goes mad. "The world it pictures has fallen prey to lawlessness and depravity," argues Kracauer (82). Like *Caligari*, the film "denotes a state of chaos." The hero is "a creature of darkness devouring the world he overpowers"; he is "an omnipresent threat" that "reflects society under a tyrannical regime – that kind of society in which one fears everybody because anybody may be the tyrant's ear or arm" (83). Tyranny and chaos are inextricable, and if the close affinity of Dr. Mabuse to Hitler were not clear enough at the time, then in the sequel, *The Last Will of Dr. Mabuse* (1933), Lang "resuscitated his super criminal to mirror the obvious Mabuse traits of Hitler" (84).

Tyrant films came to an end with *Waxworks* (1924), in which a wax-museum owner employs a poet to create stories for his pieces. The poet dutifully pens disturbing tales, then dreams that he is the hounded innocent in each story. The movie signaled the end of the period in which "the harassed German mind retreated into a shell" (84). Its "interpretation of chaos and tyranny … adds the final touch to the tyrant films proper" (87) in Germany.

Tyranny was by no means the only way to seek "the foundations of the self" in the German imagination, but once it was rejected, the sole alternative presented was "chaos with all passions and instincts breaking loose." Kracauer notes sadly that from 1920 to 1924, "the *German screen never championed or even visualized the cause of liberty*" (88; emphasis added). Instead, films depicting the sway of "unchecked instincts were as current as those devoted to tyrants." In the wake of their devastating defeat in the First World War, the Germans felt themselves oscillating between Scylla and Charybdis, believing they had no choice other than that between the "cataclysm of anarchy or a tyrannical regime." In desperation, they turned to the ancient concept of Fate: "Doom decreed by an inexorable Fate was not a mere accident but a majestic event that stirred up metaphysical shudders in sufferers and witnesses alike." At this historical moment, Oswald Spengler (1880–1936) articulated what many Germans felt in *The Decline of the West, or The Downfall of the Occident* (1918–1922). He was the prophet of a decline that seemingly derived from "laws inherent in history itself" (88). In *The Myth of the State*, Cassirer attacked Spengler's work as founded on "a higher power, the power of destiny," or sheer "Fatalism," which, in turn, signaled "the rebirth of one of the oldest mythical motives." Based on "a metaphysics of history that shows all the characteristic features of myth," Spengler's historical predictions were precisely the same as "astrological prognostics."[85]

A "doom" genre arose in response. Fritz Lang's *Destiny* (1921) follows a woman desperate to reunite with her dead lover alongside three other tragic romances, set in a Middle Eastern city, in Venice, and in the Chinese Empire. The "Angel of Death and as such the agent of Fate" drops in. The plot stresses a single point: "the actions of tyrants are realization of Fate" (90).

The second movie that addresses fate is Lang's renowned *Nibelungen* (1924), which draws on the same Norse sagas and derivative medieval epic poem that inspired the "heroic" excesses of Wagner's *Ring* cycle. Lang claimed *Nibelungen* was "a national document fit to publicize German culture all over the world"; Kracauer believes this statement "somewhat *anticipated Goebbels propaganda*" (92; emphasis added). In the movie, fate is manifested in "the actions of tyrants"; within the "fate-conditioned story" (93), absolute authority asserts itself "by arranging people under its domination in pleasing designs. This can also be seen in the *Nazi regime which manifested strong ornamental inclination in organizing the masses*" (94; emphasis added). For example, *Triumph of the Will*, the 1935 Nazi propaganda film directed by Leni Riefenstahl, chronicles the 1934 Nazi Party Congress in Nuremberg, attended by more than 700,000 Nazi supporters, and proves that "*in shaping their mass-ornaments the Nazi decoration drew inspiration from* Nibelungen" (95; emphasis added). Even in the realm of choreography, Nazi Germany "carried out what had been anticipated by her cinema from its very beginning" (272).

A further genre emanating from *Caligari* Kracauer called "instinct films." Emphasizing "the surge of disorderly lust and impulses in a chaotic world," they were based mostly on Carl Mayer's scripts and "laid in a

[85] Cassirer, *Myth of the State*, 290.

lower middle-class world which is the meaningless remnant of the disintegrated world," full of "greed and jealousy" supplemented by "deep social resentment and inherited moral impulses that have lost any vital function" (96–97). These people are "instinct-possessed denizens of a shattered universe." Mayer uses them to reveal "the destruction and self-destruction they necessarily bring about." In them all, "doom is laid in the working of Fate" (97).

The Last Laugh (1924) is the most notable example of this genre. Proud of his position, responsibilities, and uniform, a hotel doorman is shocked to find out that he has been demoted to washroom attendant. Humiliated, the old man struggles to carry on with his life. The movie "implies that authority, and authority alone, fuses the disparate social spheres," yet the doorman's fall with his "uniform representing authority is bound to provoke anarchy." Although the tenants feel "alienated from the upper world with which they commune through the uniform," eventually, all "evil lower middle-class instincts are unleashed against the porter" (100).

At this point in his study, Kracauer introduces a rare, moving personal statement. He speculates that whoever "lived through those crucial years in Germany will remember the craving for a spiritual shelter which possessed the young, the intellectuals" (107). He cites "the mountain films," which sought to spread "the gospel of proud peaks and perilous ascents" (110). They exhibited a unique heroism, although later, it was "rooted in a mentality kindred to Nazi spirit" (112). Kracauer's highly ideological, teleological approach is clearest in his treatment of the *Bergfilme* released in the 1920s. Some critics describe the genre as indigenous to Germany, comparable to the American Western. However, Kracauer claimed, "The surge of pro-Nazi tendencies during the pre-Hitler period could not better be confirmed than by the increase and specific evolution of the mountain films." They showed "the horrors and beauties of the high mountains," in particular "majestic cloud displays" (257) that would subsequently appear in the opening scene of Riefenstahl's *Triumph of the Will*. In filming "Hitler's airplane on its flight" to the 1934 Nazi Party Congress, it became "the ultimate fusion of mountain cult and Hitler cult" (258). Kracauer concludes that the "*bulk of the German people could not help submitting to Hitler*," perhaps taking tyranny, doom, and helplessness—or hypnotism and somnambulism in the movies—a bit far (272. Emphasis added).

Inevitably, then, the movies' attempt to resolve the unbearable inner dilemma between tyranny or chaos resulted in "the resumption of authoritarian behavior, presupposing a mentality that would prefer even a tyrannical regime to chaos." In the immensely popular *Fridericus Rex* series, "the psychological course leading from the rebellion of the crown prince to his final submission is strongly emphasized" (117); the moral lesson of the films was clear: "to submit unconditionally to absolute authority" (118). They announced that the seeds of Nazism were planted in the early years of the Weimar Republic.

Another film advocating authoritarian behavior was *The Street* (1923). One night, a middle-aged man, desperately longing for sensation and splendor, is lured away from his happy home by the thrills and dangers of the modern city streets. The city is an expressionistic nightmare, a dangerous and chaotic place, where the unfortunate man encounters thieves, prostitutes, and other predators. After many adventures, he returns home and "willingly submits to the domestic regime" (120). Like *The Cabinet of Dr. Caligari*, Kracauer argues, *The Street* is an example of Germany's "general retreat, symptomatic of the postwar period" (120). More specifically, it reveals that "the middle-class German's reluctance to emancipate himself originated in the fear of losing not only his social privileges, but also those multifaceted potentialities he thought he had discovered within himself" (123). What can be inferred from the "figures of Frederick and the philistine" is that "powerful collective dispositions urged the resumption of authoritarian behavior" (124).

The Stabilized Period, 1924–1929

With the stabilization of the Deutsche Mark, payment of reparations, and incorporation into the financial system of the Allies, German life assumed a degree of normality, and "soon the inflation seemed a remote nightmare." This period lasted until 1929, when "the crash put an end to false prosperity." While it lasted, no one listened to the "Hitlerites," and they sank into oblivion, not so much because the Weimar Republic was strong, but because the "abundance of foreign loans ... helped reduce unemployment" (131). Drawing on his findings in *The Salaried Masses*, Kracauer argued that from 1924 to 1928 "the white-collar developed into an important social stratum," yet instead of acknowledging "their proletarian existence, they endeavored to maintain their middle-class status." Three-and-a-half million employees were "mentally shelterless." They filled the cities and "belonged nowhere." Nevertheless, because of their crucial position in the social structure, "much depended on their reactions," and the "*films would have to take notice of them*" (132; emphasis added).

Overall, these social, economic, and political changes made a significant impact on the film industry. With normality resumed, "the fantastic figures and unreal settings of the postwar screen dissolved into thin air." Films "turned toward our world, shifting the emphasis from apparitions to actual appearances, from imaginary landscape to natural surroundings. They were essentially realistic," (184) by contrast to the "unique *monologue intérieur*" of the previous period (60). Despite this realist tendency, Kracauer was quick to point out, the films indicated that "*the outcome of the desperate struggle for psychological adjustment was a general strengthening of old authoritarian tendencies.*" He viewed the "masses" as "basically authoritarian-minded when they entered the stabilized period." The Weimar regime may have "rested upon democratic principles that repudiated those mass tendencies," but it prevented people from finding "an outlet … too persistent to yield, *authoritarian dispositions fell into a state of paralysis.*" The "decline of the German screen" in this period "is nothing but the reflection of a widespread paralysis" (137; emphasis added).

Kracauer divides the films of the stabilized period into three groups: the first testifies to "the existence of a state of paralysis"; the second sheds light on the "tendencies and notions that are paralyzed"; and the third reveals "the inner workings of the paralyzed collective soul." As a whole, they are characterized by "indifference" and "an atmosphere of neutrality" (138). Many of them reflected "society's state of paralysis," "ignored social reality," and revealed an "escapist tendency" (139–40). In *Tartuffe* (1925), based on Molière's comedy, "the paralysis was all-pervading" (147). In contrast to the 1664 original about a hypocrite who ostentatiously feigns virtue, especially religious virtue, the movie, "far from bringing home hypocrisy to the audience," rather "flattered an audience anxious to leave things in the depths untouched" (148). Likewise, in Fritz Lang's *The Spy* (1928), the master spy "indulged in the spy business for the sole purpose, it seems, of spying." The film "reflected the neutrality prevalent during this period" (150).

The second group reflected "the psychological contents then paralyzed." A new version of *The Student of Prague* (1926) "put more emphasis on the psychological significance of the plot" and was a huge success. It showed that the Germans "realized their own duality, which during the stabilized period deepened the latent conflict between republican institutions and paralyzed authoritarian dispositions" (153).

The influential science-fiction film *Metropolis* (1927), set in a futuristic dystopia, is a further example. In this movie, wrote Kracauer, "the paralyzing collective mind seemed to be talking with unusual clarity in its sleep" (162). Maria, the female protagonist's demand that the heart mediate between hand and brain "*could well have been formulated by Goebbels*," who "too appealed to the heart – in the interest of totalitarian propaganda" (164; emphasis added). His argument is not far from the truth; Goebbels told Lang that he and Hitler saw the movie on its release and were very impressed; hence, "immediately after Hitler's rise to power," Goebbels sent Lang the message that Hitler wanted him "to make Nazi pictures" (164).

The new realism in this period revealed "the workings of the paralyzed collective soul," characterized by "cynicism, resignation, disillusionment." In sum, "a mentality disinclined to commit itself in any direction" (165). Characters are "reluctant to ask questions, to take sides." Kracauer quotes a contemporary: "We have lost the power of faith, and since the wheels of the world-mechanism seem to move on their own impetus, we accustom ourselves to living without trust or a feeling of responsibility" (166). The new age of disillusionment is evident in *The Joyless Street* (1925), which depicts Vienna in the aftermath of World War I. The drastic deterioration of its social conditions due to the severe economic crisis and inflation are wreaking havoc on the lives of millions. Emphasizing "the pauperization of the middle class," the movie portrays slum residents struggling to survive the depredations of greed and exploitation. The ruin of a bourgeois family depicted with such unflinching realism shocked audiences; England "prohibited public showing of the movie" (167).

The final section in "The Stabilized Period" is entitled "Brief Reveille," referencing the military signal to awaken. The 1928 Reichstag election was "an overwhelming victory for the so-called Marxist parties" (190). The republican regime seemed firmly established, yet paralysis continued to rule on screen. In fall 1929, when the New York stock market crashed, "the stabilized period came to a definite close" (208). With German industry shrinking and widespread unemployment, the concomitant political and social crisis reinvigorated the "danger of a barbaric underworld latent in German civilization as its necessary complementary product."[86]

[86] Georg Lukács quoted in Reed, *Thomas Mann*, 385.

The Pre-Hitler Period, 1930–1933

The Great Depression had profound effects on American society, but its impact on Germany was even more dire. The US loans that had propped up the Weimar economy since 1924 ceased. In 1932, German industrial production had fallen to just 58 percent of its 1928 level. The effect was spiraling unemployment. By the end of 1929, around 1.5 million Germans were without a job; within a year, this figure had more than doubled, and by early 1933, a staggering 6 million (26 percent) were out of work. The withering impact on German society included food shortages, yet millions lacked the means to obtain food when it was available. Thousands of children died of malnutrition and hunger-related diseases. Millions of industrial laborers –in 1928, the best-paid blue-collar workers in Europe—spent a year or more in idleness. In this period, wrote Kracauer, "Berlin resounded with demonstrations, and there rose to the surface sinister individuals reminiscent of mediaeval figures." In the 1930 Reichstag elections, the Nazi party dramatically increased its share of seats from 12 to 107 of the overall 577. "S. A. [*Sturmabteilung*, or Assault Division] uniforms became ubiquitous; the noise of street assaults mingled with the dissonance of musical saws" (203). As in the last act of a Greek tragedy, the prophetic visions of calamity and doom that "had been anticipated in the movies came to life" (272). The movies, so it transpired, had projected reality.

The movies Kracauer discusses in the last section of the book replaced the films that had served "as a dreamlike outlet" for "paralyzed authoritarian dispositions." Now, "the paralysis had subsided." Instead, all kinds of leanings, "authoritarian or otherwise, were at liberty to manifest themselves," and once again, "*the German screen became a battleground of conflicting inner tendencies.*" Germany's economic and political crisis sparked an intellectual and aesthetic crisis that is clearly evident in the movies made at that time. Two are noteworthy: *The Blue Angel* (1930) and *M* (*Murderer Among Us*, 1931). Kracauer considered them "a statement on the psychological situation of the time" that "penetrated [the] depths of the collective soul" (215; emphasis added).

The Blue Angel was based on Heinrich Mann's prewar novel *Professor Unrat (Professor Garbage*,1905), which caricatured the middle- and upper-class educational system of Wilhelmine Germany as well as the double standards of its titular character. In Kracauer's typology, *The Blue Angel* "vigorously resumes postwar tradition, marking the definite end of the paralysis" (218). As a rather sadistic sex story, it illustrated, like *The Street*, "development from rebellion to submission," but added "a new problem of German immaturity": the "sadistic cruelty" of its mostly middle-class characters "results from the very immaturity which forces their victim into submission." The film "*implies a warning, for these screen figures anticipate what will happen in real life a few years later*" (218; emphasis added).

The other pre-Hitler movie is Fritz Lang's *M* (1931). Lang told Kracauer that the original title was *Murderer Among Us*, but it aroused great antagonism—"'Murderer among us': the [Nazi] Party feared to be too compromised." On the day he learned that, Lang added, "he came of age politically" (219).

M depicts Berlin's hysteria after several children are murdered and during the ensuing manhunt, mustering both police and criminals, to stop the killer. Germany had been plagued by mass murders, most sensationally a series of child murders in Düsseldorf. In a 1931 article, Lang explained:

> The epidemic series of mass murders of the last decade with their manifold and dark side effects had constantly absorbed me, as unappealing as their study may have been. It made me think of demonstrating, within the framework of a film story, the typical characteristics of this immense danger for the daily order and the ways of effectively fighting them ... The film *M* should be a document and an extract of facts and in that way an authentic representation of a mass murder complex.[87]

In Kracauer's view, the movie realizes the portents of previous movies during the Weimar period, and the murderer "belongs to an old family of German screen characters," like "Baldwin in *The Student of Prague*, who also succumbs to the spell of his devilish other self," or "a direct offspring of the somnambulist Cesare" in *The Cabinet of Dr. Caligari*, who "lives under the compulsion to kill" (221). The insanity reflected in these postwar films is renewed and reinvigorated at the beginning of the 1930s: "in the wake of retrogression" following the social and economic crisis, wrote Kracauer, "terrible outbursts of sadism are inevitable." Created only a few years before the Nazi revolution, *The Blue Angel* and *M* "bear upon the psychological situation of those crucial years and *both anticipated what was*

[87] See "Fritz Lang's M: The Restored Version of the Classic 1931 Film," August 25, 2013; http://www.openculture.com/2013/08/fritz-langs-m-watch-the-restored-version-of-the-classic-1931-film.html/.

to happen on a large scale unless people could free themselves from the specters pursuing them" (222. Emphasis added).

From 1930 to 1933, the "menace of Nazi domination was felt throughout Germany" (247). Toward the end of this period, "many anguished young unemployed were so unbalanced that one evening they could be swayed by a communist spokesman and the next succumb to a Nazi agitator's harangue." During this hectic and extremely charged period, when "what remained of the German republic was about to collapse," Fritz Lang's *The Last Will of Dr. Mabuse* (1933) appeared, "*a sort of last-ditch stand against impending disaster*" (248; emphasis added). If the similarities between Dr. Mabuse and Hitler were not clearly spelled out in *Dr. Mabuse, The Gambler* (1922), then here Lang "*resuscitated his super criminal to mirror the obvious Mabuse traits of Hitler*" (84; emphasis added).

When the movie reached New York audiences in 1943, Lang wrote a "Screen Foreword," expounding his original intentions with regard to the relationship between Hitler and criminal madmen. It fully supports Kracauer's overarching thesis about the connection between films and history. This film:

> was made as an allegory to show Hitler's processes of terrorism. Slogans and doctrines of the Third Reich have been put into the mouths of criminals in the film. Thus I hope to expose the masked Nazi theory of the necessity to deliberately destroy everything which is precious to people ... Then, when everything collapsed and they were thrown into utter despair, they would try to find 'help' in the new order. (248)

It was "true," Kracauer agreed, "that the film foreshadows Nazi practices" (248). Not only intellectual studies were confronting Nazism; perhaps movies raised a more immediate warning. He went further to observe that life "under a terror regime could not be rendered more impressively." Throughout the movie, "the imminence of doom is sensed and no one knows when and where the ax will fall." However, he also maintained that "*it is hard to believe that average German audiences would have grasped the analogy between the gang of screen criminals and the Hitler gang*" (249; emphasis added). He doubted not only the audience but also the director; he felt that the movie "lacks a broad moral significance," and, "as so often with Lang, the law triumphs and the lawless glitters." Overall, he concedes that this "anti-Nazi film betrays the power of the Nazi spirit *over minds insufficiently equipped to counter its peculiar fascination*" (250; emphasis added).

In the end, Kracauer undermines his own thesis about the inextricable connection between movies and history; for if the "average German audiences" were unable to understand the meaning of the Weimar movies, and their minds were "insufficiently equipped to counter" their "peculiar fascination," (249–50) then how could films have contributed so greatly and directly to the rise and triumph of Nazism? Moreover, given the audience's and director's shortcomings, how could German films, as Kracauer claimed time and again, expose "the German soul" (3).

Epilogue

Numerous critics have faulted Kracauer's reading of the history of German films. According to Hermann Kappelhoff, "Kracauer's book gives us a view of cinema as part of the politics of aesthetics," while his biographer Gertrud Koch argued that he engaged in the "aestheticizing of politics."[88] In this, he was not alone. Cassirer and Popper politicized philosophy in *The Myth of the State* and *The Open Society and Its Enemies*, respectively; Mann politicized the novel with *Doctor Faustus*; Auerbach politicized philology and literary criticism in *Mimesis*; Hans Baron politicized the Italian Renaissance. These and other intellectual exiles from Nazi Germany were, in Walt Whitman's words, "Language-shapers on other shores,"[89] or rather thought-shapers: writing allowed them to convey to the world from their insider perspective precisely why the Nazi regime threatened all human values.

Many also found Krakauer's analysis simplistic and anachronistic—he read history backward, *ex post facto*. He searched Weimar films for signs, portents, of the *telos*—the impending horror of Nazi triumph. "Kracauer told the history of German film from the vantage point of its present end, and the present end was, in his case, the Third Reich."[90] In his *a posteriori* approach, Hitler is the climactic event, and all previous history is used (indeed, abused) to explain it. His retrospective analysis of history strives

[88] Kappelhoff, *The Politics and Poetics of Cinematic Realism* (New York: Columbia University Press, 2015), 69; Koch, *Siegfried Kracauer*, 76.

[89] *Leaves of Grass*, ed. W. Blodgett and S. Bradley (New York: New York University Press, 1965), 18.

[90] Koch, *Siegfried Kracauer*, 77.

to find shadows, seeds, origins, types, and omens of the crisis of Nazism and the Nazi revolution of 1933. Kracauer described himself as "a doctor who is performing an autopsy and at the same time doing a cross-section of a piece of his own past, which is now completely dead."[91]

Again, in this he was not alone. Cassirer in *The Myth of the State*, Horkheimer and Adorno in *Dialectic of Enlightenment*, Auerbach in *Mimesis*, and other writers of the period likewise strove to explain how the "waves of history"[92] led to the deep trauma of Nazism that drove all of them into exile. They did not propose the so-called Whig interpretation of history, an ill-constructed historiographical approach that presents the past as an inevitable progression toward liberty and enlightenment, culminating in modern forms of liberal democracy. Instead, they based their interpretations on the *crisis mode of historical thought*, the view that harrowing moments, or major turning-points, direct the course of history toward decline rather than progress. Walter Benjamin expressed this idea beautifully in "Theses on the Philosophy of History," describing thus the "Angel of History": "His face is turned toward the past. Where we perceive a chain of events, he sees one single catastrophe which keeps piling wreckage upon wreckage and hurls it in front of his feet."[93]

Kracauer's view of German films as pervaded and perverted with ominous omens of the catastrophe to come also clearly recalls Jewish and Christian prophetic interpretations of history based on a typological, teleological view that events have a meaning, a well-defined order, and a purpose that will be fulfilled in the course of time. While Kracauer does not conceive Weimar films as sacred prophetic texts such as the Old and New Testaments, he identifies types and figures in them that he considers harbingers of a doom soon to be realized in historical events. Since Germany "carried out what has been *anticipated* by her cinema," he argued, "conspicuous screen characters now came true in life itself" (272; emphasis added). German history is the embodiment of events and characters from Weimar cinema because these films revealed German psychological dispositions that crucially influenced the course and progress of German

[91] Kracauer, "Letter to Erwin Panofsky," May 21,947, quoted in Moltke, *Curious Humanist*, 96.

[92] The concept of "the waves of history" is taken from Erich Auerbach, *Mimesis: The Representation of Reality in Western Literature* (1946; Princeton: Princeton University Press, 2003), 197–98.

[93] Benjamin, "Theses on the Philosophy of History," in *Illuminations*, trans. Harry Zohn (New York: Schocken, 1969), 257–58.

history: "*It all was as it had been on the screen. The dark premonitions of a final doom were also fulfilled*" (272; emphasis added).

The search for the roots of Nazism in German films informs Kracauer's analysis throughout. *Die Nibelungen*, directed by Austrian Fritz Lang, the "master of darkness," in 1924, "anticipated" Goebbels's propaganda (92), and Lang's ideas of futuristic urban dystopia in *Metropolis* "could well have been formulated by Goebbels" (164). Likewise, he sees in Lang's *M* and von Sternberg's *The Blue Angel* "the terrible outburst of sadism" and "what was to happen on a large scale unless people could free themselves from the specters pursuing them" (222). In sum, in the films made between the wars, Kracauer detected "motifs that *supposedly* already belong to Nazi culture, which *supposedly* enjoy an essential affinity with elements of Hitlerism."[94] Such an approach forces unjustified, awkward juxtapositions of persons, events, objects, or customs from different periods, such as placing *Die Nibelungen* alongside Goebbels's propaganda. Ultimately, since Kracauer aggressively seeks to expose the horrors of Nazism at the nadir of Western humanist civilization, the end justifies the means.

Furthermore, he applies the same inextricable connections between movies, psychology, and prophecy to predict Germany's colossal defeat and devastating failure. At the very end of the book, Kracauer writes: "Battles roared and victory followed victory. It all was as it had been on the screen. *The dark premonitions of final doom were also fulfilled*" (272; emphasis added), as in the case of *The Cabinet of Dr. Caligari* and *The Last Will of Dr. Mabuse*.

German movies reflected the Nazi flight from reason and reality: "during the postwar years most Germans eagerly tended to withdraw from a harsh outer world into the intangible realm of the soul" (67). The British poet and novelist Stephen Spender wrote in 1945 that barbarism had become the rule of the day and "brought nearly all those things which we hold firm and sacred into danger and collapse: truth and humanity, reason and right. We lived in a possessed world. For many of us the result was not unexpected when the insanity of a day broke out into delirium in which this poor European humanity sank back, fanatical, stupefied and mad."[95] Thomas Mann observed that the Nazis "entered the arena of history proclaiming themselves bearers of a barbarism that, while wallowing in ruthlessness, was to rejuvenate the world." He claimed that the "very defi-

[94] Quaresima, "Introduction," xxxviii; emphasis original.

[95] Spender, *European Witness* (New York: Renal & Hitchcock, 1946), 231.

nition of Germanness [is] a psychological state threatened by the poison of loneliness, by eccentricity, provincial standoffishness, neurotic involution, unspoken Satanism."[96] The Weimar films provide a vivid picture of these awful specters of barbarism and demonism embedded within the German soul.

Kracauer's socio-psychological method also drew criticism. One critic wrote that it was too narrow and "overly influenced" by his "personal circumstances" as an exile from Nazi Germany.[97] Another called *From Caligari to Hitler* "the most simplistic, mechanical application of psychoanalysis,"[98] and yet another claimed it was based on overt "simplification"; for example, the contention that "Germans are retrogressive adolescents predestined by character structure to political dictatorship."[99]

The themes of tyranny and chaos that dominate Kracauer's perspective and his conspicuous neglect of the influence of German Romanticism on *The Cabinet of Dr. Caligari* in particular and German Expressionist cinema in general also raise serious concerns. One of Kracauer's earliest correspondents wrote: "The motif of tyranny vs chaos is not *specifically* characteristic of the period after" World War I. "It characterized likewise the 1810-1830 period." He notes that E. T. A. Hoffmann's psychological horror story *The Sandman* (1816) bears many similarities to *The Cabinet of Dr. Caligari*, and urged Kracauer "to bring out the *specific* characteristics of the 1920s as contrasted with the 1820s,"[100] or the late eighteenth- and early nineteenth-century German Romanticism of the Brothers Grimm, Hoffmann, von Kleist, even Goethe.

Times of great danger determine both the modes of conviction and persuasion and the politics of interpretation and representation. The words of the German historian Leopold von Ranke (1795–1886) about the battlefield may be applied to ideological and cultural struggle: "War, Heraclitus tells us, is the father of all things. Out of the conflict of opposing forces, in the great moment of danger, disaster, resurgence, and

[96] Mann, *Doctor Faustus*, 184, 326.

[97] Quaresima, "Introduction," xli.

[98] Remzszhardt, quoted by Quaresima, "Introduction," xl.

[99] L.M. Hanks, Jr., "*From Caligari to Hitler*: A Psychological History of the German Film," *Journal of Aesthetics & Art Criticism*, 6, 254 (December 1947): 174.

[100] Richard Krautheimer to Kracauer, July 1944, quoted in Elsaesser, *Weimar Cinema*, 66–72.

deliverance, new developments proceed most decisively."[101] As for Kracauer, he was a survivor, pursuing an essential mission that gave meaning to his life in exile. He strove to reveal how decisively the Weimar films had contributed to the *Eclipse of Reason*, the title of Horkheimer's 1947 book. Kracauer was deeply immersed in his subject and felt compelled to relate in great detail the horrors and terrors that appeared on the Weimar screen and were fully realized under Nazism.

Kracauer's book is rich in texture and density; like the movie about Caligari, it fascinates us because it is a moving personal testimony embodying the contradictions of the Weimar Republic. Its virtues should not blind us to its faults, especially his simple, linear, teleological, deterministic history based on demonic or helpless characters and incidents of horror and terror that unfold in close sequence. Like Mann in *Doctor Faustus*, Kracauer could convey his experience only in an apocalyptic history revealing omens that gradually expose the descent, as both heritage and fall, of the German soul. Again, as in Mann's work, apocalypse and eschatology are the central themes: history as a disclosure of something hidden in the German soul, leading to a final conflagration. In clear contrast to the Apocalypse of St. John, in which the New Babylon is permanently destroyed and replaced by the New Jerusalem, heaven on earth, Kracauer and Mann see nothing beyond imminent doom and destruction. *From Caligari to Hitler* may be rightly seen as a prolog to *Doctor Faustus.*

Finally, since Kracauer's ultimate aim is to show how Weimar cinema foretold the tyranny, terror, and horror to come, he is "quite selective in his choice of examples" and left out many films of the period. For example, "he pays almost no attention to comedy directors such as [Ernst] Lubitsch or Reinhold Schünzel." His ideologically oriented choices include "roughly 8 per cent of the films made during the years 1919-33 and ... no more than 25 per cent of the films that have survived."[102] For a study that purports to reveal German identity and history during the Weimar Republic, this approach is obviously tendentious. Instead of a "psychological history of the German film," Kracauer wrote a grand *Kulturkampf* against Nazism and fascism, the forces that drove him into traumatic exilic displacement. A 1947 reviewer was not too far from the

[101] von Ranke, "Universal Tendencies," in *Leopold von Ranke, The Secret of World History: Selected Writings on the Art and Science of History*, ed. Roger Wines (New York: Fordham University Press, 1981), 150.

[102] Elsaesser, *Weimar Cinema*, 30, 32.

truth when he argued that "*From Caligari to Hitler* looks very much like a refugee's revenge."[103] In 1941, before his departure from France to the United States, Kracauer wrote to his friend Theodor Adorno mentioning, "eight years of an existence that does not deserve the name."[104] He had every reason to wage a fierce, unmitigated *Kulturkampf* against the forces that drove him into exile.

From Caligari to Hitler: A Psychological History of the German Film is built on three pillars: psychology, Weimar films, and the Weimar Republic. In the end, they merge in one eschatological and apocalyptic *crescendo*—a Satanic prophecy about the imminent doom and destruction of the liberal, humanist Weimar Republic and the establishment of Nazi Germany. The films under discussion exposed terrible signs, figures, and portents of the coming disaster. They brought to light deep psychological dispositions that came to predominate the German soul from 1918 to 1933 and influence the course of history: "*many motifs known from the screen turned into actual events*" (272; emphasis added). *Caligari* opened the Pandora's Box of the German soul, letting many evils and sins escape to find concrete expression in the Nazi world. Characters and events in the movies "now came true in life itself," and dreadful, apparitions "walked about in flesh" (272). Kracauer's study of the latent prophesy of the German screen recalls the powerful message of Goya's etching, "The Sleep of Reason Produces Monsters."

[103] Eric Bentley, "The Cinema: Its Art and Technique," *New York Times Book Review*, 18 May 1947.

[104] von Moltke, *Curious Humanist*, 2.

Erich Neumann and the Western Crisis of Ethics

Erich Neumann's *Depth Psychology and a New Ethic* (1949) was written in response to the Holocaust. He endeavored to distill psychological insights from the crisis of the twentieth century. The old Judeo-Christian morality, he argued, represses evil and led to the horrific phenomena such as Nazism and Fascism, and thus lost its power to deal with modern problems.

Instead, he formulated a new ethic that accepts darkness and one's negative traits, instead of the old ethic, which is based on perfection. By providing a psychological interpretation of the vicissitudes of his time, Neumann initiated nothing less than a Copernican Revolution in psychology, which lay the foundation for a new form of human solidarity on the ruins of World War Two.

Introduction

> This book [*Depth Psychology and a New Ethic*] … was conceived during the Second World War and under its direct impact … (Neumann, *Depth Psychology* (19))

In 1942, nine years after he left Nazi Germany in 1934 and migrated to Palestine, Erich Neumann began to write *Depth Psychology and a New Ethic* (*Tiefenpsychologie und Neue Ethik*, 1949).[1] He was living in Tel Aviv

[1] Depth Psychology refers to approaches to therapy that focus on the exploration of the subtle, unconscious, and transpersonal aspects of human experience. A depth approach may

A. Zakai, *Jewish Exiles' Psychological Interpretations of Nazism*,
https://doi.org/10.1007/978-3-030-54070-8_5

when reports arrived that Panzer Army Africa (*Panzerarmee Afrika*) under Field Marshal Erwin Rommel had begun the second phase of its advance toward Egypt, aiming to take control of the oilfields of the Middle East, Persia, and even Baku on the Caspian Sea. Given that the horrors of the Holocaust were already common knowledge, the small group of Jewish settlers in Palestine could only expect the worst. At this crucial existential moment, when Rommel was "at the door," as Neumann wrote, he began work on *Depth Psychology*, seeking to reveal the psychological causes and factors that led to the triumph of Nazism and the horrors of the Second World War and the Holocaust. He endeavored to distill psychological insights from the crisis of the twentieth century, upon which he would formulate his depth psychology to usher in a new ethic.

Neumann set out to provide a psychological interpretation of the vicissitudes of his time, the Age of Catastrophe in Eric Hobsbawm's words. Neumann was by no means the only German intellectual exile to leverage his specific discipline and expertise in an attempt to explain modern Western history. Many fellow exiles from Nazi Germany, mostly Jews, drew on their various disciplines as they strove to define, reveal and explain the course and decline of Western history in general, and the horror of the Nazi Revolution in particular: Max Horkheimer and Theodore Adorno employed sociology in their *Dialectic of Enlightenment* (1944, revised 1947); Leo Strauss turned to political philosophy in *Natural Right and History* (1953); Erich Auerbach delved into philology in *Mimesis: The Representation of Reality in Western Literature* (1946); Ernst Cassirer's analysis in *The Myth of the State* (1946) rests on philosophy; Karl Popper's on political philosophy in *The Open Society and Its Enemies* (1945); Erich Fromm employed psychology in *Escape from Freedom* (1941), and Thomas Mann sought answers in the realm of literature in *Doktur Faustus* (1947).

Neumann employed Jungian concepts to formulate the core arguments at the heart of his book, especially the archetype of the "shadow," the

include therapeutic traditions that explore the unconscious, and involves the study and exploration of dreams, complexes, and archetypes. During the 1930s, before writing *Depth Psychology*, Neumann spent most of his time writing a two-volume study on *The Origins and History of Jewish Consciousness*, which was never published. The first volume was titled *Contributions to the Depth Psychology of the Jewish Man and the Problem of Revelation*, and the second *Hasidism and Its Psychological Relevance for Jewry*. See, Martin Liebscher, "Uncertain Friends in Particular Matters: The Relationship between C. G. Jung and Erich Neumann," in *Turbulent Times, Creative Minds: Erich Neumann and C. G. Jung in Relationship (1933–1960)*, eds. E. Shalit and M. Stein (Asheville, NC.: Chiron, 2016), 27.

animal side of our personality (reminiscent of the id in Freud), through which he strove to explain the horrors and upheavals of the twenty century. The Judeo-Christian "old ethic" pursued an illusory perfection by repressing the "shadow," he argued; hence it lost its power to deal with modern Western problems. More seriously, by repressing evil it leads to horrific phenomena such as Nazism and the Holocaust. By contrast, Neumann offers "a new ethic," whereby every individual must accept the evil within him or her. Rather than casting it off and repressing it, they should learn to live with it, sometimes even to manifest it, and to pay the price in the currency of sorrow and guilt feelings.

Convinced that the deadliest danger confronting humanity is "scapegoat" psychology associated with the old ethic, Neumann used Carl Jung's "shadow" archetype, or "shadow aspect/archetype," to show that this scapegoat psychology produces the most disastrous effects on the life of the collective in the form of wars and the extermination of minority groups that do not hold mainstream opinions. Scapegoating led to a campaign of annihilation waged under the pretext of upholding morality against evil in the person of one's neighbor. The only alternative to this shadow projection and its disastrous consequences lies in its recognition, and its integration with the totality of the self.

The goal of the new ethic is therefore to achieve wholeness rather than perfection. This is the core of Neumann's "new ethic," which envisions a new human condition based on human consciousness as well as the collective unconscious, which extends right down to the animal level. His is a new human standpoint that accepts darkness and one's negative traits. By invoking the thing that we have in common as human beings, the shadow, Neumann throws a rope across the divide that has brought so many horrors in modern history. He initiated a Copernican Revolution in psychology; Depth Psychology discovered the "essence of human nature" and revealed "the structure of human nature," which "everywhere, in essence, is the same." Accordingly, Neumann points to the ways and means to achieve the solidarity of the human race or the "brotherhood of man." Acknowledging the shadow as the basic, common dimension in human beings should enhance human solidarity. Humanity, he argued, has no other option but to huddle closer together if it was to hold its own against the shadow's tyrannical power. Neumann's New Ethic's ultimate goal, therefore, is to lay the foundation for a new form of human solidarity on the ruins of World War Two.

Neumann's Life and Thought

The Jewish question … touched us deeply in our hearts. (Gerhard Adler[2])

Meeting with you always brings me a substantial affirmation that cannot be found anywhere else in the world. (Neumann to Carl Jung, Oct. 11, 1958)

Erich Neumann (1905–1960) was a psychologist, philosopher, writer, and a student of Carl Jung (1875–1961), the Swiss psychiatrist and psychoanalyst who founded Analytical Psychology. He was born in Berlin to a Jewish family. The philosopher and historian Gershom Scholem, a close friend of Neumann, remarked that his "Jewish identity was profound and unequivocal."[3] Likewise, Neumann's childhood friend Gerhard Adler (1904–88), a leading figure in the world of Analytical Psychology known for his translation into English and editorial work on The Collected Works of C. G. Jung, wrote that "the Jewish question … touched us deeply in our hearts."[4]

Neumann studied at the University Berlin, where he took courses in psychology, philosophy, and others fields (1923–26). In 1926 he moved to Nuremburg to complete his studies of philosophy and psychology at the Friedrich-Alexander-Universität Erlangen-Nürnberg. He wrote a dissertation on the mysterious language philosophy of Johann Arnold Kanne (1773–1824), the German philologist and linguist, who developed a method of "speculative etymology" in which he sought to find the one primordial mythology from which all others sprang. During his time in Nuremburg, Neumann wrote a commentary on Kafka's *The Castle* (German: *Das Schloss*), as well as fifteen short stories, which he sent to Martin Buber (1878–1965), the Austrian-born Jewish philosopher best known for his philosophy of dialogue. Subsequently, Neumann's interest in psychoanalysis and psychotherapy led him to study medicine at the Friedrich-Wilhelm-University in Berlin. He completed his studies there in

[2] Gerhard Adler, quoted in Martin Liebscher, "Introduction," in *Analytical Psychology in Exile: The Correspondence of C. J. Jung and Erich Neumann*, ed. Martin Liebscher, Trans. Heather McCartney (Princeton: Princeton University Press, 2015), p. xii. Hereafter cited as *Analytical Psychology in Exile*.

[3] See Gershom Scholem's obituary for Erich Neumann, at http://www.erelshalit.com/2014/07/gershom-scholem-obituary-for-erich.html

[4] Liebscher, "Introduction," in *Analytical Psychology in Exile*, xii.

1933 but was barred from undertaking an internship given the implementation of the Nazi race laws.

It was in Berlin in 1933 that Neumann first met Carl G. Jung at a seminar Jung was conducting in Berlin. Jung was fifty-seven years old and already renowned for his own brand of psychotherapy. The two men started a correspondence that would continue up until Neumann's death in 1960.[5] Neumann noted that for him their correspondence was like "an 'analytic session,'"[6] constantly referring to Jung as "my inner leader."[7] Neumann admitted that he was a compulsory writer—"It is truly a type of compulsion and addiction – I have been writing almost constantly since my twelfth, certainly since my sixteenth year." This was definitely, he continued, "part of my nature," although "it sometimes seems to be a true paper hell."[8]

Lifelong Zionists, Neumann, his wife Julia, and their little son Micha, left Nazi Germany for good in 1933. They traveled first to Switzerland where Neumann spent six months of analysis with Jung, while young Micha and his mother migrated to Palestine in 1934. Erich followed them several months later. The family settled in Tel Aviv in 1934, where Neumann established himself as a Jungian analyst and began writing in German about his Jewish experience and Jungian ideas, while keeping up a lifelong correspondence with Jung. Eventually he would become the founding father of analytical psychology in the future state of Israel. For years he regularly returned to Zürich, Switzerland, to deliver lectures at the C. G. Jung Institute. He also lectured frequently in England, France, and the Netherlands, and was a member of the International Association for Analytical Psychology and president of the Israel Association of Analytical Psychologists. He practiced analytical psychology in Tel Aviv from 1934 until his death in 1960.

In his long correspondence with Jung, Neumann constantly referred to his sense of isolation, loneliness, solitude and remoteness in Palestine, and later the state of Israel. "My isolated work here makes the slow but not interminable rhythm of my life more audible to me," he wrote to Jung in 1935, "so you must, please, not lose patience with me as I will also not

[5] An instructive discussion of Jung and Neumann's correspondence can be found in Nancy Swift Furlotti, "Companion on the Way: Conscious in Conflict," in *Turbulent Times, Creative Minds*, 45–69.

[6] Neumann to Jung, Nov. 15, 1939, in *Turbulent Times, Creative Minds*, 153.

[7] Neumann to Jung, July 26, 1950, ibid., 267.

[8] Neumann to Young, Dec. 28, 1953, ibid., 301.

do."[9] In 1937 he complained about "isolation that is only barely compensated for by work. Apart from my wife … no one here" in Tel Aviv "understands anything of these things" of Analytical Psychology.[10] In 1947 he went so far as to declare that no "one knows how torturous the isolation is in which we live here."[11] In 1950 he wrote to Jung about his "state of remote isolation" and "enforced isolation."[12]

During his youth, Neumann had searched for his Jewish roots. He was deeply intrigued by Martin Buber's writings on Hassidism and Hassidic Judaism, a pietistic Jewish religious movement centered around renewal and spiritual energy, that emerged in eastern Europe during the eighteenth century. It was led by a mystical rabbi, Israel ben Eliezer (also called Baal Shem Tov, 1698–1760), widely considered to be the founder of Hasidism. Neumann believed that ben Eliezer and his successor, the Mezritcher Maggid (Rabbi Dov Baer ben Avraham of Mezeritch, 1704–1772), had found a transparency between the outer and the deeper realities, enabling them to see *through*, to perceive the Divine element in the world.[13] According to Lance Owens, who wrote about the longstanding relationship between him and Jung, Neumann apparently found in the Swiss psychiatrist and psychoanalyst the *tsaddik* (a Hasidic righteous, spiritual master, leader and guide.) His was the search for a unique spiritual leader who was able to see the world in a similar way. No wonder that after his six months of analysis with Jung, Neumann affirmed for the remainder of his life that this had been *the* transformative event of his life and he could not imagine what his life might have been like without that experience.[14] "Meeting with you," he wrote to Jung in 1958, "always brings me a substantial affirmation that cannot be found anywhere else in the world."[15] Over the years Neumann's admiration of Jung reached new heights; Jung's analytical psychology he argued was "the bearer of a new consciousness of humanity for modern man," and as such he was "the

[9] Neumann to Jung, October 10, 1935, ibid., 114.

[10] Neumann to Jung, July 23, 1937, ibid, p. 131.

[11] Neumann to Jung, Feb. 1, 1947, ibid., 178.

[12] Neumann to Jung, July 26, 1950, ibid., 266–7.

[13] See, http://www.depthinsights.com/blog/the-c-g-jung-erich-neumann-connection-an-interview-with-dr-lance-owens/ On Neumann and Hasidism, see Tamar Kron, "Erich Neumann and Hasidism," in *Turbulent Times, Creative Minds*, 367–83.

[14] See, http://www.depthinsights.com/blog/the-c-g-jung-erich-neumann-connection-an-interview-with-dr-lance-owens/

[15] Neumann to Jung, October 11, 1958, in *Analytical Psychology in Exile*, 342.

healer of modern man."[16] With the outbreak of World War in 1939, the correspondence between Jung and Neumann was abruptly cut off, to be resumed in 1945 after the war was over.

When Neumann and Jung reconnected after World War Two, Jung was deeply appreciative of the way that Neumann had creatively applied depth psychology. He showered praise on *Depth Psychology and a New Ethic*, which focused on encountering the shadow in ourselves that we see in the "other."[17] One of the reasons that Jung lauded this study was that both he and Neumann felt that humanity was on the verge of a great transformation following the Second World War. Later, when Neumann sent Jung a copy of *Origins and History of Consciousness* (*Ursprungsgeschichte des Bewusstseins*, 1949), an exploration of the mythological stages in the evolution of consciousness, such as the creation myth and the hero myth, Jung deemed it 'brilliant.'

Carl Jung's Influence on Erich Neumann

> Jung's analytical psychology [is] the bearer of a new consciousness of humanity for modern man. (Neumann, *Depth Psychology* (140))

> Jung appears as the healer of modern man ... and places himself on the side of humanity, on the side of the creature – and on the side of the shadow. (Neumann, *Depth Psychology* (140))

The Swiss psychiatrist and psychoanalyst had a crucial, decisive influence upon Neumann. Not only did Neumann undergo psychoanalysis with Jung in Zurich, but their life-long correspondence clearly reveals that Neumann regarded his letters to Jung "a bit too much like an 'analytic session.'"[18] One of the sources of Jung's influence on Neumann was his personality theory. Jung believed that Sigmund Freud's concept of the unconscious was limited. Instead of simply being a reservoir of repressed thoughts and motivations, as Freud believed, Jung argued that the unconscious could also be a source of creativity. By far the most important

[16] Neumann, *Depth Psychology and a New Ethic* (London: Hodder and Stoughton, 1969 [1949]), 140. All references in the text are to this edition.

[17] Neumann's book "caused harsh reactions and criticism in Zurich." See Martin Liebscher, "Uncertain Friends in Particular Matters: The Relationship between C. G. Jung and Erich Neumann," p. 27.

[18] Neumann to Jung, Nov. 15, 1939, in *Analytical Psychology in Exile*, 153.

difference between Jung and Freud is Jung's notion of the collective, or transpersonal unconscious. This is Jung's most original and controversial contribution to personality theory, denoting the level of unconscious shared by all human beings, which comprises latent memories from our ancestral and evolutionary past. As Jung wrote: "The form of the world into which [a person] is born is already inborn in him, as a virtual image."[19] According to this psychological personality theory, the human mind has innate characteristics "imprinted" on it as a result of evolution. These universal predispositions stem from our ancestral past. Fear of the dark, or of snakes and spiders, might be clear examples. More important, however, than isolated tendencies are those aspects of the collective unconscious that have developed into separate sub-systems of the personality. Jung called these ancestral, primordial memories and images archetypes. They are the "structural elements of the collective unconscious."[20]

Archetypes, Jung believed, are images and thoughts that have universal meanings across cultures, which may show up in dreams, literature, art or religion. These symbols from different cultures are often very similar because they have emerged from archetypes shared by the entire human race. For Jung, therefore, our primitive past becomes the basis of the human psyche, directing and influencing present behavior. Jung purported to have identified a large number of archetypes but paid special attention to four of them. The "persona" (or mask) is the outward face we present to the world. It conceals our real self and Jung describes it as the "conformity" archetype. This is the public face or role a person presents to others as someone different to who they really are (like an actor). A second archetype is the "anima/animus," which is the mirror image of our biological sex, that is, the unconscious feminine side in males and the masculine tendencies in women. Each sex manifests attitudes and behavior of the other by virtue of centuries of living together. The psyche of a woman contains masculine aspects (the animus archetype) and the psyche of a man contains feminine aspects (the anima archetype). Next is the "shadow," which is the animal side of our personality (corresponding to the id in Freud). It is the source of both our creative and destructive energies. In line with evolutionary theory, Jung's archetypes may be viewed as

[19] Jung, *Psychology and Alchemy*, in *Collected Works of C. G. Jung*, Vol. 12, trans. Gerhard Adler and R. F. C. Hull (Princeton: Princeton University Press, 1980 [1953]), 188.

[20] Neumann, *The Origins and History of Consciousness* (Princeton: Princeton University Press, 1971 [1949]), xv.

reflecting predispositions that once had survival value. (As will be seen later, the "shadow" is the locus of Neumann's *Depth Psychology and a New Ethic.*) Finally there is the "self," which provides a sense of unity in experience. For Jung the ultimate aim of every individual is to achieve a state of selfhood (similar to self-actualization) and in this respect he (like the German-born American developmental psychologist and psychoanalyst, Erik Erikson (1902–1994)) moved toward a more humanist orientation than that of Freud.

Neumann's most enduring contributions to Jungian thought are *The Origins and History of Consciousness*, and *The Great Mother: An Analysis of the Archetype* (*Die große Mutter. Der Archetyp des grossen Weiblichen*, 1955). Another work, *Depth Psychology and a New Ethic*, 1949, reflects on human destructiveness and the way the human mind relates to its own shadow. His works also elucidate the way mythology throughout history reveals aspects of the development of consciousness that run parallel in the individual and society as a whole.

In 1932 Neumann also undertook a critical study of Franz Kafka's works at a time when Kafka was still a minor figure in the literary world.

Neumann contributed to the field of developmental psychology and the psychology of consciousness and creativity, and his work has been seen as an important and enduring contribution to Jungian thought. He is best known for his theory of feminine development, a theory formulated in numerous publications, most notably his book *The Great Mother*, which deals with mother goddesses and is dedicated "To C. G. Jung, friend and master in his eightieth year."[21] The book strove to provide "a structural analysis of an archetype" and to show "its inner growth and dynamic, and its manifestations in the myths and symbols of mankind."[22]

Neumann's *The Origins and History of Consciousness* charts what he calls the "mythological stages in the evolution of consciousness,"[23] which include the creation myth, the hero myth, and the transformation myth.[24] According to the theories he proposes in this book, which were based on

[21] Neumann, *The Great Mother: An Analysis of the Archetype* (New York: Bollingen Foundation, 1963 [1955]), v.

[22] Ibid., xli.

[23] Neumann, *The Origins and History of Consciousness*, xv.

[24] The book has been described as "Jungianism at its learned best" by the critic Camille Pagilia. See Pagilia, *Sex, Art, and American Culture: Essays* (London: Penguin Books, 1993), 114. And the psychotherapist Robert H. Hopcke deemed *The Origins and History of Consciousness*, along with *The Great Mother*, "Neumann's most enduring contribution to

his study of creation myths from around the world and his clinical experience, human consciousness develops out of the unconscious through a series of stages, a process represented by the ego's emergence from a primordial condition of self-contained unconsciousness symbolized by the circle of a snake devouring its own tail.[25]

Depth Psychology and a New Ethic: Historical Context

> The lake of blood which swallowed Europe and threatens to engulf the entire world. (Neumann, *Depth Psychology* (25))

> The problems that compelled me to [write] this work ... was Rommel at the door. (Neumann to Jung, May 25, 1957[26])

> *New Ethic* was an attempt to process a series of phantasies that roughly corresponded timewise with the extermination of the Jews, and in which the problem of evil and justice was being tossed around me. (Neumann to Jung, June 14, 1957)

Jungian thought." See Hopcke, *Jung, Jungians and Homosexuality* (Boston: Shambhala Publications, 1989), 70–72.

[25] Neumann's *The Origins and History of Consciousness* received very critichars hal criticism. The philosopher Walter Kaufmenn singled out Neumann's book as a "perfect illustration" of the "utterly tedious, pointless erudition coupled with a stunning lack of even elementary concern with objections and alternatives" that distinguishes "most of the literature on archetypes and the collective unconscious." Furthermore, according to Kaufmann, *The Origins and History of Consciousness* is "quintessentially dogmatic and operates with a notion of evidence not far different from the tracts of theologians who 'prove' points by citing a few Biblical verses that are far from proving what they claim. He is delighted when he finds something 'in Syria, Asia Minor, and even in Mesopotamia.' Diffusion is never even considered as an alternative explanation." See, Kaufmann, *Discovering the Mind: Volume Three: Freud, Adler, and Jung. Transaction* (New York: Routledge, 1980), 353–354. The psychologist James Hillman wrote that Neumann's identification of consciousness with the "heroic-Apollonic mode" forced him into the position that consciousness is masculine even in woman, which Hillman finds absurd. See, Hillman, *The Myth of Analysis: Three Essays in Archetypal Psychology* (New York: Harper & Row, 1978), p. 289.

[26] Neumann to Jung, May 25, 1957, in *Analytical Psychology in Exile*, 324. Emphasis added.

Depth Psychology and a New Ethic, 1949, reflects on human destructiveness and the way the human mind relates to its own shadow, or the animal side of our personality. As stated on the book's back cover:

> The modern world has witnessed a dramatic breakthrough of the dark, negative forces of human nature. The 'old ethic,' which pursued an illusory perfection by repressing the dark side, has lost its power to deal with contemporary problems ... the deadliest peril now confronting humanity lay in the 'scapegoat' psychology associated with the old ethic. We are in the grip of this psychology when we project our own dark shadow onto an individual or group identified as our 'enemy,' failing to see it in ourselves. The only effective alternative to this dangerous shadow projection is shadow recognition, acknowledgement, and integration into the totality of the self. Wholeness, not perfection, is the goal of the new ethic.[27]

These most pessimistic views on the "dramatic breakthrough of the dark, negative forces of human nature" in modern history are based, inter alia, on Neumann's own existential condition in the city of Tel Aviv in Palestine. More specifically, he wrote to Jung that "the problem that compelled me to [write] this work back then in the Second World War" was "*Rommel at the door.*"[28] In North Africa during the Second World War, Panzer Army Africa (*Panzerarmee Afrika*) under Field Marshal Erwin Rommel (1891–1944) had commenced the second phase of its advance toward Egypt, and between February and May 1942, the front line stabilized near Tobruk. Rommel believed his army would soon "secure the oilfields of the Middle East, Persia, and even Baku on the Caspian Sea."[29]

Given that knowledge of the Holocaust had reached already the world, it is no wonder that Neumann and the small group of Jewish inhabitants in Palestine were deeply concerned about the outcome of Rommel's advance. This is why Neumann asserted in his letter to Jung that that his book the "*New Ethic* was an attempt to process a series of phantasies that roughly corresponded timewise with *the extermination of the Jews*, and in which the problem of evil and justice was being tossed around me."[30] Hence the new ethics in the title of the book, *Depth Psychology and the New Ethics*, refers to the fact that for Neumann "the old concept of sin has

[27] Erich Neumann, *Depth Psychology and a New Ethic*, back cover.
[28] Neumann to Jung, May 25, 1957, in *Analytical Psychology in Exile*, 324. Emphasis added.
[29] Richard J. Evans, *The Third Reich at War, 1939–1945* (New York: Allen Lane, 2008), 467.
[30] Neumann to Jung, June 14, 1957, in *Analytical Psychology in Exile*, 331. Emphasis added.

become untrue, it is no longer effective, and that is not due to the decline of man but to his new understanding of himself and God."[31] The horrors of World War II, the Holocaust, and Rommel's imminent invasion of Palestine, among others factors, led Neumann to believe that the "problem of evil is one of the most central problems of modern man." (25) Hence in his *Depth Psychology* he argued that it was imperative to break free of the "old ethic," which led one to project our own dark shadow onto an individual or a group identified as our "enemy" while failing to see it in ourselves. The only solution to this dangerous shadow projection, he maintained, was shadow recognition, which would transform the human psychological condition, and thus the human condition as a whole, by effecting an integration between a good psyche and an evil one, and hence promoting the totality of the self. The true remedy for the problem of humanity was to be found not through social or political means, but rather in the psychological sphere, through the transformation of our understanding of the human, psychological condition.

Psychology, Ethics and History

> The problem of evil is one of the most central problems of modern man … we are living in a world in which evil in man is emerging from the depths on a gigantic scale and confronting us all. (Neumann, *Depth Psychology* (25))

> The shadow side of human race towers over us all … (Neumann, *Depth Psychology* (19–20))

> The alliance between Faust and Mephisto is the alliance of modern man with the shadow. (Neumann, *Depth Psychology* (116))

Neumann's *Depth Psychology and a New Ethic* appeared in 1949. Deeply moved by the horrors of Nazism and Fascism and in reaction to the Holocaust, he strove in this book to offer a psychological solution to what had led to the catastrophe of his times in the form of a new ethics. He argued that the modern world was witnessing a dramatic breakthrough of the dark, negative forces of human nature, as evidenced in the brutal atrocities committed during his time. The origin of this modern outburst of evil and horror was to be found in the "old," Judaeo-Christian ethic,

[31] Ibid., 333.

which pursued an illusory perfection by repressing the dark side in humans, and which had lost its power to deal with acute contemporary problems. While other intellectual exiles from Nazi Germany such as Erich Auerbach, Hans Baron, and Ernst Cassirer lauded the Judaeo-Christian humanist tradition in their overall *Kulturkampf* against Nazi barbarism,[32] Neumann was highly critical of it, to say the least; hence in his book he strove to construct a new ethic based on Jungian psychological foundations.

Neumann took the Jungian archetype "shadow," or the "dark side" of the human soul, the animal side of our personality, and fashioned it into the cornerstone of his book: the "shadow side of human race towers over us all, darkening the sky with its death-rays and its atom bombers." (19–20) Ultimately, *Depth Psychology* reflects on human destructiveness and the way the human mind relates to its own shadow. Neumann was convinced that the deadliest peril confronting humanity in his times lay in the "scapegoat" psychology associated with the old ethic, which led to separation and enmity between individuals, groups, and nations. He therefore developed a revolutionary idea: Judaeo-Christian morality represses evil, leading to horrific phenomena such as Nazism. As Neumann's son Micha, a psychiatrist too, argued: "He said that every person has to accept the evil within him, not to cast it away and not to repress but to live with it, sometimes even to manifest it, and to pay the price of sorrow and guilt feelings."[33]

Persuaded that the basic problem of modern man was the problem of evil, Neumann maintained that "conventional ethics have proven incapable of containing or transforming its destructive forces."[34] His constant emphasis on the shadow, the dark side of people's souls, is not hard to understood. For his was the "Age of Catastrophe," or *historia*

[32] See, for example, Leo Strauss, *Natural Right and History* (1953); Erich Auerbach, *Mimesis: The Representation of Reality in Western Literature* (1946); Ernst Cassirer, *The Myth of the State* (1946); and Hans Baron, *The Crisis of the Early Italian Renaissance* (1966). These various cultural wars waged against Nazism and Fascism are analyzed in Avihu Zakai, *Erich Auerbach and the Crisis of German Philology: The Humanist Tradition in Peril* (Dordrecht: Springer, 2017); David Weinstein and Avihu Zakai, *Jewish Exiles and European Thought in the Shadow of the Third Reich: Baron, Popper, Strauss, Auerbach* (Cambridge: Cambridge University Press, 2017); and Avihu Zakai, *The Pen Confronts the Sword: Exiled German Scholars Challenge Nazism* (Albany: SUNY Press, 2018).

[33] See Aviva Lori, "Jung at Heart," *Haaretz*, Nov. 2017, at https://www.haaretz.com/jung-at-heart-1.148506

[34] Gerhard Adler, "Foreword to This Edition," in Erich Neumann, *Depth Psychology and a New Ethic* (London: Hodder and Stoughton, 1969 [1949]), 7–8.

calamitatum: the "decades from the outbreak of the First World War to the aftermath of the Second," when European civilization "stumble[d] from one calamity to another. And there were even times when even intelligent conservatives would not take bets on its survival."[35] Likewise, the English philosopher and historian R. G. Collingwood wrote in 1942 about "the incessant tempests through which we have precariously lived for close to thirty years," from 1914 to 1942.[36] The Hungarian Marxist philosopher, aesthetician, literary historian, and critic Georg Lukács, called it "the age of absolute sinfulness."[37] And the English poet, novelist and essayist Stephen Spender wrote in 1945 that these years and especially World War II had "brought nearly all those things which we hold firm and sacred into danger and collapse: truth and humanity, reason and right. We lived in a possessed world. For many of us the result was not unexpected when the insanity of a day broke out into delirium in which this poor European humanity sank back, fanatical, stupefied and mad."[38] As for Neumann, he too believed that he lived in "an age dominated by a dance of death." (19) In such a dark period in human history, his ultimate quest was not for a social and political remedy but rather, true to his psychological discipline, for a solution in the inner, dark abysses of the human soul. This was the foundation upon which the modern tragedy of Nazism and Fascism had played out.

What modern man needed was a true awareness of evil, above all the evil within oneself first and foremost of "his own 'dark' inferior personality, his own shadow." For this "dark," "shadow" side in man is "projected into the other person – one way of satisfying the well-known need to find a scapegoat for one's own shortcoming," as the terrible, bloody annals of modern history clearly revealed. In more practical terms, the human quest for a scapegoat leads one to split "the world into 'good' and 'bad,' superior and inferior nations, races, or individuals, with catastrophic

[35] Eric Hobsbawm, *The Age of Extremes: History of the World, 1914–1991* (New York: Pantheon, 1994), 6–7.

[36] R. G. Collingwood, *The New Leviathan: or Man, Society, Civilization, and Barbarism* (Oxford: Clarendon 1991 [1942]), lx.

[37] György Lukács, "Preface" (1962) to *The Theory of the Novel: A Historic-Philosophical Essay on the Forms of Great Epic Literature* (1920; London: Merlin, 1971), 18. See also Lukács, *The Destruction of Reason* (1962; Atlantic Highlands, NJ: Humanities Press, 1981), 714–64.

[38] Stephen Spender, *European Witness* (New York: Renal & Hitchcock, 1946), 231.

consequences."[39] Or conversely, scapegoat psychology "produces the most disastrous effects on the life of the collective" in the form of "wars and the extermination of groups holding minority opinions." (139). Here lies the intimate and inextricable association in Neumann's thought between psychology and history, or the Age of Catastrophe. He believed that man should learn "to live with his dark side" because it was an essential part of the human existential, psychological condition. This constitutes Neumann's revolutionary psychological approach: rather than suppressing, or repressing, the shadow and consequently projecting it outward, as advocated in the traditional, old Jewish and Christian ethic, "it should be integrated" within the self.[40] Only in this way could modern man achieve a fuller consciousness of his human condition, and the ambiguity of his own existence.

As did other intellectual exiles from Nazi Germany who fashioned new systems or modes of thought in response to Nazism and Fascism, Neumann too searched for a crucial starting point, a turning point in history, an *Ansatzpunkt*,[41] or a point of great epistemological departure:

> the ambiguity of one's own existence, the awareness of both positive and negative forces within the individual and the collective becomes *the point of departure* for the new ethical attitude.[42]

[39] Adler, "Foreword to This Edition," in Erich Neumann, *Depth Psychology and a New Ethic*, 8.

[40] Ibid., 8.

[41] Wilhelm Dilthey, German historian, sociologist, and hermeneutic philosopher, coined the concept of *Ansatzpunkt* in his book *Das Erlebnis und die Dichtung: Lessing, Goethe, Novalis, Holderlin* ([1914] (Göttingen: Wandenhoeck Ruprecht, 1968)).

[42] Adler, "Foreword to This Edition," 8, emphasis added. Regarding an understanding of history as based on major points of departure or turning points, see for example Max Horkheimer and Theodor Adorno, who argued in their study *Dialectic of Enlightenment*, 1944, that in the transformation from an anti-Semitic to a human society, "the Jewish question would indeed prove the *turning-point* of history." See, *Dialectic of Enlightenment: Philosophical Fragments*, ed. Gunzelin Schmid Noerr; trans. Edmund Jephcot (1944; Stanford: Stanford University Press, 2002), 165, emphasis added. In his *Mimesis: The Representation of Reality in Western Literature*, 1946 (Princeton: Princeton University Press, 2003), Erich Auerbach depicts the progress of Western literature as a series of major literary, semantic, cultural, and historical turning points described in each chapter of his study. "The procedure I have employed – that of citing for every epoch a number of texts and *using these as test cases for my ideas* – takes the reader directly into the subject and makes him sense what is at issue long before he is expected to cope with anything theoretical." See *Mimesis*, p. 556, emphasis added. See also Auerbach: "My own experience, and by that I mean not merely my

In his own words, which echoed Martin Buber's famous "I and Thou,"[43] Neumann claimed that acceptance "of the shadow is the essential basis for the actual achievement of an ethical attitude toward the 'Thou' who is outside me."[44]

The revolutionary dimension of this new ethical system should not overlooked; not only did Neumann strive to do away with the traditional, old Jewish and Christian ethic, but based his new ethic upon a conflict with traditional collective values and morals, or more generally, with Western humanist tradition founded upon shared values and beliefs about innate human goodness. According to him, the decisive ethical authority, the locus of ethical behavior, "no longer rests with collective values of good and evil and with conventional 'consciousness' but with an inner 'Voice' – a constant challenge to individual decision and responsibility, even where it may lead to *a rejection of collective morality*."[45] Neumann's new ethic may indeed be considered a Copernican Revolution in the field of ethics and morals since it shifts the core and heart of morals from the external, traditional, communal collective realm, into the dark inner abysses of the soul. His is indeed a system of ethics based on psychology; an individualistic system bereft of any historical, traditional context of morals.

The title of Neumann's book—*Depth Psychology and a New Ethic*—is indeed most appropriate. Abandoning the collective sphere of traditional,

scientific experience, is responsible for the choice of problems, *the starting points*, the reasoning and the intention expressed in my writing." This quote is taken from Auerbach's preface to his *Literary Language and Its Public in Late Latin Antiquity and the Middle Ages,*1965, trans. Ralph Manheim (Princeton: Princeton University Press, 1993), 30, emphasis added. On intellectual exiles from Nazi Germany who strove to explain history as based on major points of departure or turning points, see Zakai, *Erich Auerbach and the Crisis of German Philology: The Humanist Tradition in Peril*; Weinstein and Zakai, *Jewish Exiles and European Thought in the Shadow of the Third Reich*; and Zakai, *The Pen Confronts the Sword: Exiled German Scholars Challenge Nazism.*

[43] Martin Buber, *I and Thou* (*Ich und Du*), 1923 (Charles Scribner's Sons. 1937). One of the major themes of the book is that human life finds its meaningfulness in relationships. In Buber's view, all of our relationships bring us ultimately into relationship with God, who is the Eternal Thou. According to Buber's biographer, Professor Paul Mendes-Flohr, "Buber and Neumann knew each other and corresponded with each other. Neumann regarded himself a disciple of Buber. He wrote at least one essay on one of Buber's Hasidic stories." See Letter to the author, Nov. 11, 2017. See also, Paul Mendes-Flohr, *Martin Buber: A Life of Faith and Dissent* (New Haven: Yale University Press, 2019).

[44] Neumann as cited by Adler, "Foreword to This Edition," 8.

[45] Adler, "Foreword to This Edition," 8, emphasis added.

historical and communal values of good and evil, with its morality based on shared social and political values, he grounded his ethics solely and exclusively on the positive and negative forces within one's own existence, or the light and the shadow within the human soul. Such a radical individualist approach to ethics grants precedence and predominance to individualism. As Neumann argued, the "individual must work through his own basic moral problem before he is in a position to play a responsible part in the collective."[46] Carl Jung, who clearly recognized the revolutionary ramifications of Neumann's approach, wrote to him in 1948, after reading *Depth Psychology*, that its "effect would be like a bomb."[47]

Yet, ironically, transferring the ultimate locus and goal of ethics and morality from the public, collective sphere into the innermost abysses of the human soul, nonetheless reveals an important humanist dimension in Neumann's system. As human beings, we all share the positive and negative forces within our souls; hence, dividing the world into good and bad, superior and inferior nations, races, or individuals, loses its significance, power, and validity.

Depth Psychology and a New Ethic

> Have problems of ethics or even of a 'new' ethic any relevance at all in an age dominated by a dance of death, to which National Socialism in Germany was little more than a prelude? (Neumann, *Depth Psychology* (19))

> The ambiguity of one's own existence, the awareness of both positive and negative forces within the individual and the collective becomes the point of departure for the new ethical attitude. (Gerhard Adler, "Foreword" to *Depth Psychology and a New Ethic*, 1968)

The dark shadow of the Second World War and its unimagined horrors and atrocities hovered over *Depth Psychology and a New Ethic*, 1949, from beginning to end. "This book," wrote Neumann on the first page, "was conceived during the Second World War and under its direct impact." This was "an age dominated by a dance of death, to which National Socialism in Germany was little more than a prelude." (19) His is a Copernican Revolution in psychology that sought to show how depth

[46] Neumann as quoted by Adler, ibid., 9.
[47] Jung as cited by Adler in ibid., 9.

psychology could be used to achieve the solidarity of the human race. Neumann thus concluded his book with a grand, prophetic, cosmological vision: "mankind, gripped as it is by the icy cold of empty, lifeless, cosmic space, which stares at it horribly from every side, sans God, sans soul, and sans humanity, has no other option than to huddle closer together, if it is to hold its own against this [the shadow's] tyrant power." (135) As this indicates, the book's ultimate objective was to offer a solution to the terrible events of modern history by proposing a "new ethic" that may serve as the basis for new human solidarity.

Neumann's mission became all the more pressing in view of "the louring spectre of a third world war" and the "production of atomic bombs" By the Americans and the Russians. Ultimately, he believed that "the highest endeavor of the human species has always been devoted to the creation of the individual." Hence, in evolutionary terms, the "Community of Free Individuals is the next goal of evolution – still remote, but already visible on the horizon." (19) Such is the grand humanist goal that Neumann set himself; not a social or political agenda, but rather a purely psychological one—to place a clear mirror before the face of the human being's dark and tormented soul and to reveal its deep, evil abysses.

Neumann found the answer to the horrors of his time, to "the moral crisis of the twentieth century," (30) in "the shadow of the human race." (19) He of course was not the first to identify the crucial importance of the shadow's reign over the human soul. Before him, numerous modes of thought and religious beliefs had acknowledged the inner dark side in human beings' psyche, most notably Judaism and Christianity, and had striven to overcome it. Yet these systems had, according to Neumann, lost their power, meaning and validity in modern history. The "old religious and ethical values have lost their grip on modern man," and "he in turn has lost the grip on life which they used to give him." This is why modern man "finds himself in a position of the *gravest danger*," which appears not only "in the sick people who the psychotherapist meets in his consulting-room every day, but which equally *affects those so called normal persons who wage our wars, conduct our recurrent persecutions, and plan and prepare the necessary means for carrying these purposes into effect.*" (21, emphasis added) In a modern world "sans God, sans soul, and sans humanity," psychological problems affecting leaders of nations, as was the case with Hitler and Nazi Germany, became crucial to the welfare of human beings. Clearly, the solution to "the gravest danger" humanity faced in modern times ought to be found in the method of psychology, which among all our disciplines deals best with the "shadow of the human race." (19).

An important dimension of modernity's "grave moral crisis," argued Neumann, is the "nihilist despair about man which is an essential characteristic of the art and philosophy in our period." Nihilism was clear evidence of the decline of traditional religious and ethical modes of thought and beliefs, which in turn facilitated the horrors of the current "lake of blood which swallowed Europe." (25). Yet, in all the discussions about humanity's "gravest danger" in modern times, argued Neumann, something important was missing; "the creative capacity of man and (though this is really the same thing) the creative of the human psyche is deliberately overlooked." In response to this acute problem, declared Neumann, "depth psychology is essentially concerned with this very subject." (21).

In the Introduction to his study, Neumann pointed to the connections between the problem of evil, modern history, and the Age of Catastrophe: "The problem of evil," he asserts "is one of the most central problems of modern man." We are living in a world, he continues, in which "evil in man is emerging from the depths on a gigantic scale and confronting us all." (25)[48] Over the course of modern history, humanity mastered nature, but this period was also the time "in which man's incapacity to deal with psychic nature, with the human soul, has become more appallingly obvious than ever before." Clear evidence of such disability and its plain result was the current shedding of blood, which "is the result of this incapacity." (25) He defined the first half of the twenty century as "a collective outbreak of the evil in man, on a scale never before manifested in world history." So far all traditional ideological, political, and sociological explanations of this horrifying phenomenon had "never grasped the real cause of the matter," and "cannot explain away the fact that it has been possible for evil to seize hold of hundreds of millions of human beings."

[48] Compare these words to Ernst Cassirer's: "We are always living on a volcanic soil and must be prepared for sudden convulsions and eruptions. In the critical moments of man's political and social life myth regains its old strength. It was always lurking in the background, waiting for its hour of opportunity. This hour comes if the other binding forces of our social life, for one reason or another, lose their influence; if they can no longer counterbalance the demonic power of myth." See Cassirer, *The Myth of the State* (1946; New Haven: Yale University Press, 1967), 280. Likewise, Erich Fromm argued that people looked upon the periods before Nazism as "a volcano which for long time has ceased to be a menace." But this longstanding optimistic belief was shattered "when Fascism came into power." See, Fromm, *Escape from Freedom* (New York: Rinehart & Company, 1941), 8.

Furthermore, the "old ethic of the Judaeo-Christian epoch has proved itself incapable of mastering the destructive forces of man." (25–6).[49]

An analysis of the "the moral crisis of the twentieth century" and the horrors and atrocities which engulfed Europe is of the utmost urgency, given the fact that "the human race is in danger of being annihilated by the 'moral insanity' which has taken possession" at present and which is "a symptom of a transitional period lacking ethic." On the one hand, it was clear that "the front lines in the conflict at present dividing mankind are clearly delineated," as manifested in the political and military forces that fought in the two world wars. Yet, Neumann emphasized that "man's present state of possession by evil is a phenomenon that transcends political and military frontiers and centers into the heart of each one of us." In other words, the "murdered are also guilty – not only the murderer." (26) This was a bold conclusion that may not be accepted by the victims, say, of the Holocaust.

In order to lay the ground for his "new ethic," Neumann had to minimize and in fact indeed to erase the difference between perpetrator and victim, stating that

> Those who saw and failed to act, those who looked away because they did not want to see, those who did not see although they could have seen, and those, too, whose eyes were unable to see – each and every one of these is actually in alliance with evil. *We are all guilty – all peoples, all religions, all nations, all classes. Humanity itself is guilty.* (26, emphasis added)

This highly radicalized and relativist approach to the phenomenon of evil, placing the blame on both perpetrator and victim, could have been proposed only by someone who lived in Tel Aviv, far removed from the horrifying atrocities of the Second World War and the Holocaust.

The presence of evil is revealed not only in Nazism, but is evident also in other spheres of modern human life, such as the discrimination of black people. "The evil that broke through in the Nazi's claim to world domination is the same evil" that prevented the "solution of the social problem and self-determination of the colored people in the civilized world." This

[49] Compare Neumann's views to those of Ernst Cassirer in his book *The Myth of the State*, 1946, p. 3: "In the last thirty years, in the period between the first and second World Wars, we have not only passed through a severe crisis of our political and social life but have also been confronted with quite new theoretical problems. We experienced a radical change in the form of political thought … the appearance of a new power: the power of mythical thought."

is the very evil that attempts "with all its might to destroy the reality of the unity of mankind and the consciousness of single destiny for culture and human race." (26).

Yet the question remains, how may we confront this evil that seeks to "destroy the reality of the unity of mankind"? Clearly not by political or social means, according to Neumann and his depth psychology. Today the "people of our time are in an unenviable position" because "they have nothing with which to confront the deliberate annihilation of the world by evil except an ethic," namely the Jewish and Christian ethic, "which has already lost its psychological efficacy." Consequently, without an efficient alternative means modern man is "an easy prey to infection" by evil:

> The inner insecurity of the individual who relies on the values of the old Judaeo-Christian ethic, but no longer feels its validity in his heart and experiences its impotence in his everyday life renders him an easy prey to infection. (27)

There is, asserted Neumann, evidently an urgent need for a new ethic to replace the old one, which was based on an illusory sense of perfection achieved by repressing the dark side in humans. One of the grave consequences of the old ethic was that it led to "scapegoat psychology, in which the individual eliminates his own evil by projecting it on to the weaker brethren," as evident in modern nationalism. (130) Or, conversely, by projecting our own dark shadow onto an individual or groups identified as our "enemy," and failing to see it in ourselves. The only possible psychological response to this was a clear acknowledgement of both the positive and negative sides in human beings, a new awareness, a shadow awareness, which would lead to its integration into the totality of the self. This is the foundation of Neumann's "new ethic."

In the past "the 'old' ethic in its Judaeo-Christian form molded the character of Western man." Yet its loss of efficacy was "the cause, the effect and the expression" of the present "catastrophe," (28), or "the crisis of the twentieth century." (30) In order to confront it, argued Neumann, "the study in depth of the psychological development of the individual in whom the problem of evil becomes manifest is in a much better position than any research into collective events to detect those first attempts at synthesis which are the basic elements of a new ethic." For in order to survive at all, the individual needs "the aid of the forces of the deep conscious; in them and in himself he may be able to find new ways, new forms of life, new values and new guiding symbols."(29) Neumann thus transferred the problem of evil, which confronts modern man in both the collective and individual spheres as revealed in the vicissitudes of contemporary history, from external historical events and human actions and deeds to the deep abysses of the individual's conscious and un-conscious. This was depth psychology's radical psychological solution to the horrors of modern history.

Faithfull to the premises of Jungian psychology, Neumann argued that the reality of evil by which the individual is possessed does not derive merely from his personal circumstances: "it is also, at the same time, the individual expression of a collective situation;" namely, "the creative side of the collective – that is, universal human – unconscious." (29) The individual thus became the center, the scepter, of the collective history of consciousness and unconsciousness, and could thus through his agency provide the solution to "the moral crisis of the twentieth century." In other words, "the creative stirrings which enable him to find his own solutions and salvation are the initial stage of future values and symbols for the collective." (30) Here lies the intrinsic, essential connection between the psyche and the course of history, for the "future of the collective lives in the present of the individual." (30) The connection, then, between "the problems of the individual and those of the collective is far closer than is generally realized." For each single individual "is an organ of the collective, whose common inner structure he bears in his collective unconscious." (31).

The scope of the old ethic "comprises the most variegated human ideals and includes a whole gamut of degrees of perfection," involving ultimately an assertion of "the absolute character of certain values which are represented by this old ethic as moral 'oughts.'" In such an old-fashioned moral system the ideal of perfection "can and ought to be realized by the elimination of those qualities which are incompatible with this perfection." (33) Neumann strives not to examine the validity of values as such, but rather "to study the psychological effects of this old ethic on Western man." (34).

Two basic principles "made possible the implementation of the old ethic"—suppression (*Unterdrückung*) and repression (*Verdrängung*). The first, the action of suppressing, denotes "the deliberate elimination by ego-consciousness of all those characteristics and tendencies in the personality which are out of harmony with the ethic value;" namely, "the denial of the negative." Its clearest manifestations are "discipline and asceticism."

As such suppression is "a conscious achievement of the ego, and it is usually practiced and cultivated in a systematic way." Through it "a sacrifice is made which leads to suffering." (34) Repression, on the other hand, the action of subduing someone or something, is "the instrument most frequently used by the old ethic to secure the imposition of its values." Repressed contents, unlike those that are suppressed, "are withdrawn from the control of consciousness and function independently." As such, according to depth psychology, "*they lead to an active underground life of their own with disastrous result for both the individual and the collective.*" (35, emphasis added).

The conscious, Neumann emphasized, "is the representative of the collective norm, and changes its content and demand." (36) In this context, suppression and repression "are the two main techniques employed by the individual in his attempt to achieve adaptation to the ethical ideal." Now, the inevitable outcome of this attempt is "*the formation of two psychic systems in the personality.*" The first is "the shadow," which usually remains "completely unconscious, while the other develops into an essential organ of the psyche, with the active support of the ego." This other is the "persona." The persona corresponds to "one's adaptation to the requirements of the age, of one's personal environment, and of the community." (37, emphasis added). By contrast, those qualities, capacities, and tendencies that do not harmonize with the collective values—everything that shuns the light of public opinion—comes "together to form the shadow, *that dark region of the personality which is unknown and unrecognized by the ego.*" In other words: "The shadow is the other side. It is the expression of our own imperfection and earthliness, the negative which is incompatible with the absolute values." (40, emphasis added). As this clearly indicates, Neumann's is a Manichean psychology, based on an elaborate essential dualism with regard to the content and form of the human soul. The struggle between the good and the evil psyche is a contest between two opposite and contrasting aspects of the individual.

Neumann argued that "the ego has repressed the shadow side and lost touch with the dark contents, which are negative and for this reason split off from the conscious sector." (40) In the process the ego became the "good conscious," living in harmony with the values of its culture. But this led "the individual to forget his shadow." The ramifications of this process in relation to modern history are momentous. For forgetting the shadow fostered "Western man's illusory self-identification with positive values," which reached its highest with the "bourgeois epoch," that was "now coming to an end" with the advent of the Second World War. (41) There was, therefore, a crucial and inextricable link between the shadow and the horrors and terror of history. Ironically and sadly, Neumann argued that,

> The positive belief in progress was one of the precursors of the First World War, and the arrogation of modern man, regarding himself as the meaning and evolutionary culmination of creation, was a prelude to the bestial arrogation of the Aryans *herrenvolk* [master race] under National Socialism. (42)

What emerged from these sad historical events is the fact that "mankind [was] confronted" with the problem that "the world, nature and the human soul are the scene of a perpetual and inexhaustible rebirth of the evil." (46) Proof of this can be found in "the *projection of the shadow*." Given that the shadow "is in conflict with the acknowledged values," it "cannot be accepted as a negative part of one's own psyche and is therefore projected – that is, it is transferred to the outside world and experienced as an outside object." Instead of being treated as "one's own inner problem," it is "combated, punished, and exterminated as 'the alien out there.'" Thus the old ethic's "*elimination of these feelings of guilt and the discharge of the excluded negative forces is in fact one of the gravest perils confronting mankind.*" The clear outcome of such a psychological phenomenon is "the institution of scapegoat," (50, emphasis added) or "scapegoat psychology," through which the individual eliminates his own evil by projecting it onto the weaker part of society.(130).

Suppression and repression, the denial of the negative, thus lead to the "*scapegoat psychology*," which "shapes the inner life of nations just as it does their international relationship." More specifically,

> The unconscious psychic conflicts of groups and masses find their most spectacular outlets in epidemic eruption such as wars and revolutions in which the unconscious forces which have accumulated in the collective get the upper hand and "made history." (50–1)

Given that for the individual "evil cannot be acknowledged as 'his own evil' at all," no wonder that "evil is invariably experienced" by him "as something alien, and the victims of shadow projection are therefore, always and everywhere, the aliens." There is, then, a close link between the psyche, the soul, and the horrors of modern history, based on the premises of the old ethic, which culminates in Nazism and mass murder. For in the "economy of the psyche, the outcast role of the alien is immensely important as an object of the projection of the shadow." (52).

In sum, declared Neumann, "no war can be waged unless the enemy can be converted into a carrier of a shadow projection, and the lust and joy of warlike conflict ... is derived from the satisfaction of the unconscious shadow side." For Neumann, then, "*wars are the correlative of the old ethic, and warfare is the visible expression of the breakthrough of the unconscious shadow side of the collective.*" (58, emphasis added) Here lay the basis for Neumann's ultimate quest to shape and construct a new ethic on the foundation of depth psychology. For as a psychologist he saw the entire world solely and exclusively in terms of mental characteristics and believed that its fabric was determined by psychological problems and solutions.

The New Ethic and Its Blessing

> The shadow, that dark region of the personality which is unknown and unrecognized by the ego. (Neumann, *Depth Psychology* (40))

> Wars are the correlative of the old ethic, and warfare is the visible expression of the breakthrough of the unconscious shadow side of the collective. (Neumann, *Depth Psychology* (58))

After considering the shortcomings of the old ethic, Neumann turned to examine the content and form of the new ethic. He argued that over the course of the last 150 years, namely since 1800, or the Age of Enlightenment, we may observe "the *breakthrough of the dark side* into Western consciousness." He refers to "the discovery of the primitive element in human nature," which provided man with new perspectives on his origins. It showed him, moreover, "the dark soil in which his roots are embedded" and "radically destroyed his godlike nature" and "unmasked his central position in the universe as an illusion." (82) This important process of human beings' disenchantment from their illusion of occupying the highest place in the order of creation can be attributed, among others, to Charles Darwin, Biblical criticism, Friedrich Nietzsche's *Beyond Good and Evil*, and Sigmund Freud's *Future of an Illusion*, and to the parallel processes of secularization, materialism, empiricism, and relativism. In "no previous epoch of human history," argued Neumann, "has the dark side occupied the foreground of attention to such an extent as it does today."

(83) The clear result of this dark historical process was that "ugliness, dissonance and evil are now forcing their way into art"—in music, literature, painting. And not only in the case of Fyodor Dostoevsky, "in whose work man – sick, evil, and abandoned – stands naked at the very heart of despair," but also "detective stories, crimes, films and thrillers belong to the same uncanny context." (83).[50]

Yet, the outburst of darkness in modern times was not only perilous but "also contained the germs of any possible future development in the West." (84) Indeed, the breakthrough of the dark side was "most clearly exemplified in National Socialism," where "faith in dogma, the leader and the redeemer" led to "disintegration of individual consciousness" and the "insanity of the collective." (88) By contrast, however, in the new ethic the "only person who is morally acceptable" is "the person who has accepted his shadow problem – the person, that is to say, who has become conscious of his own negative side." (91) This important and crucial inner, emotional transformation came about thanks to the tools of psychology, since "the unconscious is often, if not always, a more powerful determinant in the life of a man than his conscious attitude, his will and his intentions." (92) The new ethic therefore "rejects the hegemony of a partial structure of the personality, and postulates the total personality as the basis of ethical conduct." (92) It was born under "the ruling star of the fuller insight, deeper truth and cleared-sighted awareness of human nature as a whole which is the real achievement of depth psychology." (93).

Given that the moral problem of the individual was "constellated in the first place by the coexistence of ego and shadow," the personality could now become "conscious of its shadow problem;" hence, we may deal more adequately with the vicissitudes of history by understanding their psychological determinants. (93) For Neumann believed that both "the individual and the community" must be "conscious of both the positive and the negative forces" of the individual (94) Here one finds the crucial and inseparable connection between depth psychology and the course and progress of history:

> My own shadow side is a part and a representative of the shadow side of the whole human race; and if my shadow is anti-social and greedy, cruel and

[50] Horkheimer and Adorno too argued in their *Dialectic of Enlightenment* that the Age of Enlightenment led to the rise of the myth of power, and, eventually, to "the reversion of enlightened civilization to barbarism in reality." *Dialectic of Enlightenment*, p. xix.

> malicious, poor and miserable – if he approaches me in the form of a beggar, a negro or a wild beast – then my reconciliation with him will involve at the same time my reconciliation with the dark brother of the whole human race. (95)

Acknowledging one's dark side is the cornerstone of depth psychology's therapeutic solution for modern man. Furthermore, living in peace with the shadow brings the ego to "its solidarity with the whole human species and its history as known in subjective experience." This encounter leads one, moreover, to become better "conscious of group psychology," and to appreciate that "the conscious mind" is only a small part of the "whole vast universe of the psyche." For what is specifically "human and individual only constitutes the topmost layer of *the collective unconscious which extends right down to the animal level.*" (96, emphasis added).

The social and political consequences of acknowledging one's dark, shadowy side are tremendous: depth psychology and the new ethic required the assimilation of "the primitive side of our own nature before we can arrive at a stable feeling of human solidarity and co-responsibility with the collective." In more practical terms, and more closely related to modern human beings' psychological, existential condition, from the acceptance of the primitive side it follows that

> *the projection of this component will cease, and together with it the psychology of the scapegoat and the campaign of annihilation waged under the pretext of morality against evil in the person of one's neighbor.* (97, emphasis added)

Building upon these contentions, Neumann proceeded to formulate a psychological law, according to which the "instability of a group or individual varies directly with the extent of the area occupied by unconscious contents and inversely with the scope of the consciousness." This law "can be verified everywhere and in everyone," Neumann argued, and he stressed time and again that since "primitive and mass psychology are to be found deep-rooted in each individual," these have direct, serious and tragic consequences on modern history. (98).

The New Ethic's Aims and Values

Depth Psychology and a New Ethic envisions a new human condition based on human conscious as well as "the collective unconscious which extends right down to the animal level." While the old ethic was founded upon "partition, differentiation and dichotomy, as formulated in the mythological projection of the Last Judgment under the image of the separation of the sheep from the goat, the good from evil," the ideal of the new ethic, on the other hand, "is the combination of the opposites in a unitary structure." (101) Its goal is "the achievement of wholeness, of the totality of the personality," or the integration of "the two systems of the conscious mind and the unconscious." Neumann likened the totality of personality to the "League of Nations," established in 1920: "ego-consciousness becomes the locus of responsibility for a psychological League of Nations, to which various groups of states belong, primitive and pre-human," and so forth. Its hallmark is that "the assimilation and use of the negative forces to be found in every psychic system takes place as far as possible consciously, within the process of self-realization." (102).

Neumann's glorious vision of the new ethic rests upon the "basic tasks of modern man," out of which aroused a "new human standpoint which accepts darkness and the negative side." It is likewise founded upon the view that modern man "has reacted to the collapse of the anthropocentric cosmos with a shift in emphasis toward super-personal human values and the brotherhood of man which is becoming clearer every day." (134)[51] This grand cosmological vision resembles Friedrich Schiller's "Ode to Joy" (*An die Freude*, 1785), which declares that:

> What convention strictly divides;
> All people become brothers.

[51] It is very interesting to compare Neumann's vision of the "brotherhood of man" with the invention of Esperanto by the Polish-Jewish physician and ophthalmologist L. L. Zamenhof (1859–1917). Zamenhof became fascinated by the idea of a world without war and believed that this could come about with the help of a new international auxiliary language, Esperanto, which he first developed in 1873. See Esther Schor, *Bridge of Words: Esperanto and the Dream of a Universal Language* (New York: Metropolitan, 2016); and Joan Acocella, "Return to Babel: The Rise and Fall of Esperanto," *The New Yorker*, Oct. 31, 2016, 90–5.

This highly optimistic, utopian view of the brotherhood of mankind, which clearly had no relation to reality, could be formulated only after the horrors of the Second World War. Neumann himself stressed this point repeatedly. For he believed that Depth Psychology had found the "essence of human nature." It exposed the "limitation of the human condition," which "must inevitably lead, in the course of the next few centuries, to an increased sense of human solidarity." This was so because "*the structure of human nature is everywhere, in essence, the same.*" Or, conversely, the different archetypal constellations notwithstanding, "*the human species is nevertheless one and indivisible in the basic structure of its mind.*" (134–5, emphasis added) Clearly, the psychologist had turned into an utopian visionary, offering a psychologist's solution to the problems of history, a remedy that was far removed from human beings' real and actual life and experience.

Neumann was happy to reveal, through the tool of depth psychology, the common structure and essence of human nature and the human mind. Hence, at the end of his book he allowed himself to express highly cosmic speculations, not only about the "solidarity of our species" but also about "the unity of our planet." Just as the solidarity of our species "accounts for the inner history of mankind," so the "unity of the planet earth will determine the history of the future." (135) Depth psychology, then, has serious implications not only for the human soul, but also for the future of the human race.

Neumann's *Depth Psychology* lays out a grand psychological utopia of the human race, written in response to Nazism. For slowly "but surely, the human race is withdrawing the psychological projections by means of which it had peopled the emptiness of the world with hierarchies of gods and spirits, heavens and hells; and now, the amazement, for the first time, it is experiencing the creative fullness of its primal psychic Ground." (135) Thus ends the book, which was born in the "lake of blood which swallowed Europe" during the Second World War, with a powerful cosmological utopian vision pertaining to the solidarity of the human race. This was no small feat for an exiled scholar who had witnessed his beloved Western humanist tradition going up in smoke and many of his relatives and friends murdered during the Holocaust.

Like many utopian ideals over the centuries, which tend to emphasize egalitarian principles of equality in economics, government and justice, Neumann's *Depth Psychology* championed the egalitarian principles of a unified, common human psychological system. Based on Depth

Psychology, he initiated a Copernican Revolution in psychology that discovered the "essence of human nature" and "the structure of human nature," which "everywhere, in essence, is the same." This discovery led him to proclaim the basic, essential solidarity of the human race, or the "brotherhood of man," contrary to the ethos, for example, of Nazism and Fascism. Understanding that the shadow was the basic, essential common dimension of human beings' life and experience would lead eventually to an enhanced human solidarity. In the face of the horrors and brutality of modern history, Neumann argued that humanity had no other option but to huddle closer together, if it were to hold its own against the shadow's tyrannical power.

Yet, as with so many other grand utopian visions over the centuries, history constantly and relentlessly refuted these utopian dreams, and it was rather the dark, destructive nature of human beings that revealed itself throughout time and history.

Epilogue

Recent decades have witnessed a surge of important studies dealing with intellectuals' confrontation with fascism and Nazism, and the societal roles that they can play, especially during such "dark times." This is an area that is close to my study, and it is therefore important to mark the difference between some of these studies and mine in terms of content and form and with regard to the meaning and significance intellectuals assigned to their works.

Sean Forner's *German Intellectuals and the Challenge of Democratic Renewal*[1] offers a highly original exploration of a network of antifascist intellectuals. This fascinating study surveys a range of scholars and journalists, such as Karl Jaspers and Alfred Kantorowicz, who spent the German occupation years (1945–1949) rethinking democracy in postwar, post-Nazi Germany and crafting intellectual support for a new democratic society. The book examines how democracy was restructured in Germany in the wake of National Socialism, the Second World War and the Holocaust. My study, by contrast, seeks to locate the marrow, content and form of Nazi psychology by examining works of four German-Jewish scholars who, in their exile, sought to probe the pathology of the Nazi soul. The psychology of the Nazi phenomenon, then, rather than the renewal of democracy, was their ultimate goal.

[1] Cambridge, Cambridge University Press, 2014.

A. Zakai, *Jewish Exiles' Psychological Interpretations of Nazism*,
https://doi.org/10.1007/978-3-030-54070-8_6

Udi Greenberg's highly acclaimed, award-winning, *The Weimar Century: German Émigrés and the Ideological Foundations of the Cold War*[2] reveals the origins of two dramatic events: Germany's post-World War II transformation from a racist dictatorship to a liberal democracy, and the ideological genesis of the Cold War. It examines, more specifically, the life and thought of the Protestant political thinker Carl J. Friedrich, Socialist theorist Ernst Fraenkel, Catholic publicist Waldemar Gurian, liberal lawyer Karl Loewenstein, and international relations theorist Hans Morgenthau. Given that the author's goal is to chart the road to building democracy, or the rise of the Cold War, he obviously does not probe the terrifying dark psychological abysses of the Nazi soul, as did the writers with whom I deal. Finally, Anson Rabinbach's book of collected essays, *In the Shadow of Catastrophe: German Intellectuals between Apocalypse and Enlightenment*,[3] deals with the writings of some key figures in twentieth-century German philosophy, such as Walter Benjamin and Ernst Bloch, and explores their ideas in relation to the two world wars and the horrors facing Europe at that time. The writers in my study had little interest in apocalypse or the Enlightenment, but rather grappled with all their might with the horrific consequences of Nazi psychology.

The four men whose ideas and theories I discuss here had much in common. They were born around the turn of the century in the German-speaking sphere into Jewish families. They studied at prestigious academic institutions and went on to explore the inner recesses of the human psyche, and they all were forced into painful exile following the Nazis' rise to power in Germany. This shared seminal experience drove them all to search for an explanation of the cataclysmic event that transformed their lives, and they recorded the results of their endeavor in groundbreaking influential works, which constitute major components of a broader *Kulturkampf* leveled against fascism, Nazism, and totalitarianism. It is the nature, path, and outcomes of this burning quest that I address in this book. I contend that collectively, the interpretations of these four men provide important insight into the unique psychological phenomenon of Nazism and the dialectical engendering of authoritarian tendencies.

Reich, Fromm, Neumann, and Kracauer all strove to address the same acute existential problem. Nazism and Fascism ruined their lives and destroyed any illusions they may have had about civilization and progress.

[2] Princeton, Princeton University Press, 2014.

[3] Berkeley, University of California Press, 2001.

They all believed, in Fromm's words, that "if we want to fight Fascism we must understand it."[4] Reich inaugurated psychological inquiry into the nature, source, and form of Nazism, and other exiled Jewish intellectuals followed in his path. Like Reich, Fromm and Kracauer leveraged insights from both psychology and Marxism in interpreting Nazi social and political phenomena. Again following Reich, they identified the attractions of Nazism for the German lower middle class.

Wilhelm Reich's *The Mass of Psychology of Fascism*, which appeared in 1933, was the first of the works I address here to be published. The other three were written during and immediately after World War II. Reich's study is the first attempt to explore the psychology of Nazism by assessing it as an integral part of "the social catastrophes of the twentieth century."[5] The key question that Reich explored in his book was why the German masses embraced authoritarianism even though it ran counter to their interests, and he concluded that the elements of fascist feeling and thinking were built into every individual's psyche. Fascism, therefore, was the expression of the irrational structure of the modern "mass man," which on some level led him in fact to desire fascism. Reich rejects the explanation of fascism that rests on the masses' ignorance or delusions, focusing instead on their frustrations and desires. *The Mass Psychology of Fascism* argues that emotions and desires must be taken into account: "'Fascism' is the basic emotional attitude of the depressed man of our authoritarian machine civilization and its mechanistic-mystical conception of life."[6] Reich argued that the field of mass psychology was better equipped to explain the rise and hold of fascism and Nazism than vulgar Marxist interpretations. Fascism was, in essence, the "organized political expression of the structure of the average man's character."[7] Reich furthermore traced a direct link between widespread sexual repression in modern society and the rise of fascism. Children of the proletariat, especially, learned from their parents that they must suppress almost all sexual desire, and expended their repressed energy in authoritarian idealism. Perhaps his most original contribution to the explanation of fascism and Nazism lies in the insight that the leader "can be successful...only if his personal point of view, his

[4] Fromm, *Escape from Freedom* (New York: Rinehart & Company, 1941), p. 5.
[5] Reich, *The Mass Psychology of Fascism*, xii.
[6] Ibid., xiii.
[7] Ibid., xiii.

ideology, or his program bears resemblance to the average structure of a broad category of individuals."[8]

Erich Fromm's *Fear of Freedom* (1941) was the second major work to offer a psychological interpretation of Nazism and the triumph of Fascism in particular, and the crisis of modern history in general. Like Reich, Fromm was a disciple of Freud, but eventually concluded that Freud had neglected the role of societal factors in human psychology, and came to believe that an individual's personality was the product of culture as well as biology. Fromm found the turning point toward the "escape from freedom" in the Protestant Reformation, a movement that emphasized the unworthiness of the individual, his fundamental inability to rely on himself, and his need to submit. Fromm's thesis was, essentially, that from the time of the Renaissance, the Protestant Reformation, and the dawn of capitalism, "freedom from traditional bonds of medieval society, though giving the individual a new feeling of independence, at the same time made him feel alone and isolated, filled him with doubt and anxiety, and drove him into new submission and into a compulsive and irrational activity."[9] Modern man's isolation from society, becoming a negligible "atom," and the doubts and fears that this process generates, explain how and why many seek the sanctuary and incentives of totalitarian societies. People had lost the principles that organized their lives and thus were "driven into bondage."

Like Fromm, Siegfried Kracauer had ties to the Frankfurt school and he was directly influenced by Fromm's social psychology, which illustrated that the psychological tendencies of German workers "neutralized their political tenets."[10] His major work, *From Caligari to Hitler: A Psychological History of German Film* (1947), seeks to show how German films contributed to social development and to the rise and triumph of Nazism. Films not only reflect the inner, psychological life of a nation but shape and direct it, he contended. Psychological tendencies often assume an independent life, Kracauer believed, and become "essential springs of historical evolution."[11] The title of his book reveals the intertwining of movies and history in his thought: progression from *an* incarnation of evil to *the* incarnation of evil. It is a painful, vivid, first-hand commentary on the

[8] Ibid., 36.
[9] Fromm, *Escape from Freedom*, 103.
[10] Kracauer, *From Caligari to Hitler*, 10–11.
[11] Ibid., 9.

tortured German soul, staggering between diabolic tyranny and chaos, culminating in the rise and triumph of Nazism. Among his fellow intellectual exiles, Kracauer is unique in pursuing answers in the popular media, and in his belief that movies are "cultural symbols in which the subjective characters that are developed function as markers for the collective identity."[12] Kracauer's study proposes a link between the apolitical and "escapist" orientation of Weimar-era cinema and Germany's consequent turn to totalitarianism. Film, claimed Kracauer, always reflects society; indeed, it reflects the mentality of a nation more directly than other arts. German cinema, he insisted, reflected the "satanic" side of the German soul and imagination that had emerged at a certain point in its development, and then moved ineluctably toward Hitler. Kracauer held a teleological, apocalyptic, eschatological, and deterministic view of history and read movies as prescient. Analyzing German film, he contended, would expose "deep psychological dispositions which influenced the course of events ... which will have to be reckoned with in the post-Hitler era."[13]

In the final chapter of this book I turn to Erich Neumann and his analysis of the Western crisis of ethics, as expounded primarily in *Depth Psychology and a New Ethic* (1949). Neumann was indebted to Jung, rather than Freud, and employed Jungian concepts, turning them into the core and heart of his book, especially the archetype of the "shadow," or the dark and atavistic side of the human psyche. The longstanding Judeo-Christian ethic had sought to promote perfection by repressing the "shadow," which not only stripped it of the ability to offer solutions to modern Western problems, but also led to horrific phenomena such as Nazism and the Holocaust. Thus, Neumann concluded that the problem of evil was one of the most central problems of modern man. People tended to project their own dark shadow onto other individuals or groups, thereby dehumanizing them and making them apparently legitimate targets of atrocities. Given that for the individual "evil cannot be acknowledged as 'his own evil' at all," no wonder that "evil is invariably experienced" by him "as something alien, and the victims of shadow projection are therefore, always and everywhere, the aliens."[14] Neumann sought to provide a "new ethic," according to which all people had to "accept the evil within" themselves, live with it, and integrate it into the "totality of the self."

[12] Koch, *Siegfried Kracauer*, 80.
[13] Kracauer, *From Caligari to Hitler*, li.
[14] Neumann, *Depth Psychology and a New Ethic*, 140.

Unlike the "old ethic," the goal of the new ethic was wholeness rather than perfection.[15]

Unsurprisingly, given their similar social and educational backgrounds, fields of expertise, and shared objectives, one may discern not a few links and similarities in elements of the theses that our four protagonists propounded. As mentioned, Kracauer and Fromm were all associated with the Frankfurt School, and derived insights into Nazi-era social and political phenomena from both psychology and Marxism. And Kracauer admitted that his construction of psychological history owed a great deal to "the social psychology of Erich Fromm."[16]

When Reich asserts that "twentieth-century fascism … raised the basic question of *man's character, human mysticism and craving for authority*, which covered a *period of some four to six thousand years*"; that "the abominable excesses of the capitalist era" were a direct continuation of "the human structure of the untold masses … [who had] become totally dependent upon authority, incapable of freedom"; and that "this age-old subjugation … is the essential power that drives and shapes history,"[17] one is reminded of Neumann's Jungian stereotypes and Kracauer's "deep collective psychological dispositions predominant in Germany from 1918 to 1933, the disclosure of which through the medium of the German screen may help in the understanding of Hitler's ascent and ascendancy."[18] And Reich's analysis of the destructive consequences of the repression of sexuality brings to mind Neumann's equally dire conclusions with regard to the suppression of "the shadow."

Another of Reich's original ideas was that of psychological projection, a defense mechanism through which the human ego defends itself against unconscious impulses or qualities by attributing them to others, but never to itself. Projection incorporates blame shifting. Erich Neumann uses the concept of projection in *Depth Psychology and a New Ethic*, where he argues that for the individual, evil cannot be acknowledged as "his own evil" at all, but is seen "as something alien, and the victims of shadow projection are therefore, always and everywhere, the aliens"—Jews, blacks, migrants.[19]

[15] Aviva Lori, "Jung at Heart," *Haaretz*, Nov. 2017, at https://www.haaretz.com/jung-at-heart-1.148506

[16] Quaresima, "Introduction," in *From Caligari to Hitler*, xxix.

[17] Reich, *The Mass Psychology of Fascism*, xxvi.

[18] Kracauer, *From Caligari to Hitler*, 11.

[19] Neumann, *Depth Psychology and a New Ethic*, 52.

And finally, what of the solutions that these thinkers offered humanity? How could their insightful analyses of the ills of modern society be leveraged to formulate a cure? With the exception of Kracauer, who merely remarked that Germans' deep psychological predispositions would "have to be reckoned with in the post-Hitler era," they did not shirk from putting forward bold prescriptions for a far better post-war world.[20]

In his *Depth Psychology* Erich Neumann strove, no less, to divert the awful course of modern history by offering a "new ethic" that would serve as the basis for a new human solidarity. Individuals would no longer project their own dark shadow onto another individual or group, nor use scapegoat psychology, but would recognize the shadow in themselves. This would transform the human psychological condition, and thus the human condition as a whole, because it would lead to "an integration between a good psyche and an evil one, and hence into the totality of the self." For Neumann, the core of ethical behavior was no longer to be found in the collective value of good and evil, but with an inner "voice"—a constant challenge to individual decision and responsibility, even where it may lead to a rejection of collective morality. The individual thus became the center, the scepter, of the collective history of consciousness and unconsciousness, and could through his agency provide the solution to "the moral crisis of the twentieth century."[21] In other words, "the creative stirrings which enable him to find his own solutions and salvation are the initial stage of future values and symbols for the collective." Here lies the intrinsic, essential connection between the psyche and the course of history, for the "future of the collective lives in the present of the individual."[22]

Reich's equally ambitious goal in writing *The Mass Psychology of Fascism* was to bring about change, making a plea for rationality in the midst of the tremendous irrational convulsions of the age. He asserted that "the practical problem of mass psychology is to actuate the passive majority of the population, which always helps political reaction to achieve victory, and to eliminate those inhibitions that run counter to the development of the will to freedom born of the socio-economic situation."[23] He envisaged "a possible future regulation of human society… derived not from ideologies or conditions … but from natural processes that have been present and have

[20] Kracauer, *From Caligari to Hitler*, li.
[21] Neumann, *Depth Psychology and a New Ethic*, 19.
[22] Ibid., 30.
[23] Kracauer, *From Caligari to Hitler*, 32.

been developing from the very beginning," concluding that "the discovery of natural biological work-democracy in international human intercourse is to be considered the answer to fascism."[24] His solution "is borne by the functions of love, work and knowledge and is developed organically. It fights mysticism and the idea of the totalitarian state not through political attitudes but through practical functions of life, which obey their own laws." Reich believed that fascism "can be crushed only if it is countered objectively and practically with well-grounded knowledge of life's processes."[25]

Fromm sought to pave an alternative path for his day and for ours, one contoured by love and what he called humanism. He envisaged a joyous and caring community where the love of life and the realization of everyone's creative potentialities held hegemony over the forces of repression, conformity, and destructiveness. Whereas negative freedom leads into new bondage, the possibility of "a state of positive freedom in which the individual exists as an independent self and yet is not isolated but united with the world, with other men, and nature" persists. Echoing Neumann, Fromm believed that man can achieve this "by realization of his self, by being himself."[26] Positive freedom lay in the spontaneous activity of the total, integrated personality.

In conclusion, the four studies and works I have explored and analyzed here unmistakably reveal the close and inextricable connection between history and psychology, and the extent to which psychological insights may help us explain historical phenomena, especially those related to the trauma of Nazism and Fascism. Alongside, therefore, of social, political, and economic considerations, we should take into serious account psychological factors as well, because these too drive people to action. In other words, modes of psychological inclination are essential and crucial to any explanation of modes of action and behavior throughout history.

[24] Ibid., xxvii.

[25] Ibid., xvi.

[26] Fromm, *Escape from Freedom*, 257.

Bibliography

Acocella, Joan, "Return to Babel: The Rise and Fall of Esperanto," *New Yorker*, 31 October 2016, pp. 90–95.

Adorno, Theodore, *Letters to his Parents: 1939–1951* (Cambridge, UK: Polity, 2006).

———, "The Curious Realist: On Siegfried Kracauer" (1964), in Adorno, *Notes to Literature*, ed. Rolf Tiedemann (New York: Columbia University Press, 1992).

———, *Notes to Literature*, ed. Rolf Tiedemann (New York: Columbia University Press, 1992).

———, "Wagner, Nietzsche and Hitler," *Kenyon Review*, 9, 1 (1947).

Arendt, Hannah, *The Portable Hannah Arendt* (New York: Penguin, 2000).

Auerbach, Erich, *Mimesis: The Representation of Reality in Western Literature* [1946; Princeton: Princeton University Press, 2003].

———, *Literary Language and Its Public in Late Latin Antiquity and the Middle Ages*, trans. Ralph Manheim (1965; rpt. Princeton: Princeton University Press, 1993).

Bamberger, Nathan, "A Note on Erich Fromm's Rabbinical Roots," in *Tradition: A Journal of Orthodox Jewish Thought*, 29:3 (Spring 1995), pp. 52–4.

Barnouw, Dagmar, *Critical Realism: History, Photography, and the Works of Siegfried Kracauer* (Baltimore: Johns Hopkins University, 1994).

Baron, Hans, *The Crisis of the Early Italian Renaissance: Civic Humanism and Republican Liberty in an Age of Classicism and Tyranny* (1955; Princeton: Princeton University Press, 1966).

Benjamin, Walter, "Theses on the Philosophy of History," in *Illuminations*, trans. Harry Zohn (New York: Schocken, 1969).

A. Zakai, *Jewish Exiles' Psychological Interpretations of Nazism*,
https://doi.org/10.1007/978-3-030-54070-8

Bennett, David, *The Currency of Desire: Libidinal Economy, Psychoanalysis and Sexual Revolution* (London: Lawrence & Wishart, 2016).

Berlin, "Two Concepts of Liberty" (1958), in Berlin, *Four Essays on Liberty* (Oxford: Oxford University Press, 1969).

———, *Four Essays on Liberty* (Oxford: Oxford University Press, 1969).

Binion, Rudolph, *Hitler among the Germans* (New York: Elsevier, 1976)

Blackstone, William, *The Oxford Edition of Blackstone's Commentaries on the Laws of England;* Book 4: *Of Public Wrongs* (Oxford: Oxford University Press, 2016), 53.

Buber, Marin, *I and Thou* (*Ich und Du*) (1923; rpt. New York: Charles Scribner's Sons, 1937).

Burckhardt, Jacob, *The Civilization of the Renaissance in Italy* (New York: Macmillan, 1921).

Butterfield, Andrew, "Dürer's Devil Within," at http://www.nybooks.com/blogs/nyrblog/2013/may/20/durer-devil-within/.

Cassirer, Ernst, *The Myth of the State* (1946; New Haven: Yale University Press, 1967).

———, Cassirer, *An Essay on Man: An Introduction to A Philosophy of Human Culture* (New Haven: Yale University Press, 1944), 103.

Dean, Carolyn J., *Sexuality and Modern Western Culture* (Boston: Twayne Publishers, 1996).

Deleuze, Gilles, and Guattari, Félix, *Anti-Oedipus: Capitalism and Schizophrenia* (1972; rpt. London: Continuum, 2004).

Dewey, John, *Freedom and Culture* (New York: G.P. Putnam's Sons, 1939).

Dilthey, Wilhelm, *Das Erlebnis und die Dichtung: Lessing, Goethe, Novalis, Holderlin* (1914; rpt. Göttingen: Wandenhoeck Ruprecht, 1968).

Eisner, Lotte, *The Haunted Screen: Expressionism in the German Cinema and the Influence of Max Reinhardt* (Berkeley and Los Angeles: University of California Press, 1969), 17.

Elkin, David, "Wilhelm Reich – The Psychoanalyst as Revolutionary," *New York Times Magazine*, April 18, 1971, at https://www.nytimes.com/1971/04/18/archives/wilhelm-reich-the-psychoanalyst-as-revolutionary-wilhelm-reich.html

Elsaesser, Thomas, *Weimar Cinema and After: German's Historical Imaginary* (London and New York: Routledge, 2000), 61–62.

Erikson, Erik, *Childhood and Society* (London: Imago Publishing, 1950), pp. 284–85.

Evans, Richard J., *The Third Reich at War, 1939–1945* (New York: Allen Lane, 2008).

Friedman, Lawrence, *The Lives of Erich Fromm: Love's Prophet* (New York: Columbia University Press, 2013).

Fromm, Erich, *Escape from Freedom* (New York: Rinehart & Company, 1941).

———, *The Working Class in Weimar Germany: A Psychological and Sociological Study* (Cambridge, MA: Harvard University Press, 1984).
———, *The Sane Society* (New York: Henry Holt, 1955).
Greenfield, Jerome, *Wilhelm Reich vs. the USA* (New York: Norton, 1974)
Habermas, Jürgen, *The Philosophical Discourse of Modernity: Twelve Lectures*, trans. F. G. Lawrence (Cambridge, MA: MIT Press, 1993), 106.
Hanks, L. M. Jr., "*From Caligari to Hitler*: A Psychological History of the German Film," *Journal of Aesthetics & Art Criticism*, 6, 254 (December 1947).
Hegel, Georg Wilhelm Friedrich, *Aesthetics: Lectures on Fine Art*, 1835, trans. T.M. Knox (Oxford: Clarendon, 1998).
———, *Outlines of the Philosophy of Right*, trans. T.M. Knox (1821; Oxford: Oxford University Press, 2008).
Herf, Geffrey, "Dialectic of Enlightenment Reconsidered," *New German Critique*, 117 (Fall 2012): 81–89.
Herzog, Dagmar, *Cold War Freud: Psychoanalysis in an Age of Catastrophe* (Cambridge, UK: Cambridge University Press, 2017).
———, ed, *Sexuality and German Fascism*, ed. (New York: Berghahn Boyoks, 2005).
Heym, Stefan, Ahasver (Munich: Bertelsmann, 1981).
Hillman, James, *The Myth of Analysis: Three Essays in Archetypal Psychology* (New York: Harper & Row, 1978), 289.
Hobsbawm, Eric, *The Age of Extremes: The Short Twentieth Century, 1914–1991* (London: Michael Joseph, 1994).
Hopcke, Robert H., *Jung, Jungians and Homosexuality* (Boston: Shambhala Publications, 1989).
Horkheimer, Max, and Adorno, Theodor W., *Dialectic of Enlightenment: Philosophical Fragments*, ed. Gunzelin Schmid Noerr; trans. Edmund Jephcot (1944; Stanford: Stanford University Press, 2002).
Jung, Carl, *Psychology and Alchemy*, in *Collected Works of C. G. Jung*, vol. 12, trans. Gerhard Adler and R.F.C. Hull (1953; rpt. Princeton: Princeton University Press, 1980), 188.
Kant, Emmanuel, "What is Enlightenment?" 1785, in *What is Enlightenment? Eighteenth-Century Answers and Twentieth-Century Questions*, ed. James Schmidt (Berkeley: University of California Press, 1996), pp.
Kappelhoff, Hermann, *The Politics and Poetics of Cinematic Realism* (New York: Columbia University Press, 2015).
Kaufmann, Walter Arnold, *Discovering the Mind: Freud Versus Adler and Jung* (New York: Routledge, 1981).
Koch, Gertrud, *Siegfried Kracauer: An Introduction* (Princeton: Princeton University Press, 2000).
Kirsch, Adam, "The System: Two New Histories Show How the Nazi Concentration Camps Worked," *New Yorker* (6 April 2015).

Kontje, Todd, *Thomas Mann's World: Empire, Race, and the Jewish Question* (Ann Arbor: University of Michigan Press, 2011).

Kracauer, Siegfried, *From Caligari to Hitler: A Psychological History of the German Film* (1947; Princeton: Princeton University Press, 2004).

———, *The Salaried Masses: Duty and Distraction in Weimar Germany*, trans. Quintin Hoare (1930; Verso: London, 1998).

———, *History: The Last Things Before the Last* (Princeton: Princeton University Press, 1995).

Latour, Bruno, "Why Has Critique Run Out of Steam? From Matters of Fact to Matters of Concern," *Critical Inquiry*, 30 (Winter 2004).

Lawrence, D. H., "A Letter from Germany," at http://www.newstatesman.com/europe/2013/07/d-h-lawrence-letter-germany/.

Leslie, Esther, "Siegfried Kracauer and Walter Benjamin," in *Memory: Histories, Theories, Debates*, ed. Susannah Radstone and Bill Schwarz (New York: Fordham University Press, 2010).

Liebscher, Martin, ed., *Analytical Psychology in Exile: The Correspondence of C. J. Jung and Erich Neumann*, ed. Liebscher, trans. Heather McCartney (Princeton: Princeton University Press, 2015).

Lukács, Georg, *The Theory of the Novel: A Historic-philosophical Essay on the Forms of Great Epic Literature* [1920; London: Merlin, 1971].

Mann, Thomas, *Doctor Faustus: The Life of the German Composer Adrian Leverkühn as Told by a Friend*, trans. John E. Wood (New York: Vintage, 1999).

———, *The Story of a Novel: The Genesis of Doctor Faustus*, trans. Richard Winston and Clara Winston (New York: Knopf, 1961).

———, "Germany and the Germans", in *Thomas Mann's Addresses Delivered at the Library of Congress, 1942–1949* (Washington, DC: Library of Congress, 1963).

———, *Mario and the Magician* (New York: Knopf, 1931).

———, *Letters of Thomas Mann, 1889–1955*, sel. and trans. Richard Winston and Clara Winston (New York: Knopf, 1971).

———, "Bruder Hitler," *Esquire*, 11, n. 3 (1939a), at: http://larvatus.livejournal.com/291296.html

———, "A Brother," in *Thomas Mann: Death in Venice, Tonio Kröger, and Other Writings* (New York: Continuum, 1939b).

Medoff, Rafael, "How America First Learned of the Holocaust," *Jewish News Service*, 11 June 2012, at http://www.jns.org/latest-articles/2012/6/11/how-america-first-learned-of-the-holocaust.html#.VTiUXPAauZE.

Mendes-Flohr, Paul, *Martin Buber: A Life of Faith and Dissent* (New Haven: Yale University Press, 2019).

Miron, Guy, "Judaism and Radical Thought – Erich Fromm and Leo Loewenthal during the Weimar Republic," MA Thesis, Hebrew University of Jerusalem, 1993 (in Hebrew).

Moltke, Johannes von, *The Curious Humanist: Siegfried Kracauer in America* (Oakland: University of California Press, 2016).

Mosse, George L., *Nationalism and Sexuality: Respectability and Abnormal Sexuality in Modern Europe* (New York: Howard Fertig, 1985).

———., *The Crisis of German Ideology: Intellectual Origins of the Third Reich* (1964; New York: Howard Fertig, 1998), v, 237, 243.

Mülder-Bach, Inka, "Introduction," in Kracauer, *The Salaried Masses: Duty and Distraction in Weimar Germany*, trans. Quintin Hoare (1930; Verso: London, 1998).

Neumann, Erich, *Depth Psychology and a New Ethic* (1949; rpt. London: Hodder and Stoughton, 1969).

———, *The Origins and History of Consciousness* (1949; rpt. Princeton: Princeton University Press, 1971).

———, *The Great Mother: An Analysis of the Archetype* (1955; rpt. New York: Bollingen Foundation, 1963).

Neumann, Franz Leopold, *Behemoth: The Structure and Practice of National Socialism 1933–1944* (1944; New York: Harper Torchbook, 1966).

Nicholson, Shierry Weber, "Curious Realist: On Siegfried Kracauer," *New German Critique,* no. 54, Special Issue on Siegfried Kracauer (Autumn, 1991): pp. 161.

Paglia, Camilla, *Sex, Art, and American Culture: Essays* (London: Penguin Books, 1993).

Pinkard, Terry, *Hegel's Phenomenology: The Sociability of Reason* (Cambridge: Cambridge University Press, 1994).

———, *Hegel: A Biography* (Cambridge: Cambridge University Press, 2001).

Ranke, Leopold von, *Leopold von Ranke, The Secret of World History: Selected Writings on the Art and Science of History*, ed. Roger Wines (New York: Fordham University Press, 1981).

Reed, Thomas, *Thomas Mann: The Uses of Tradition* (1973; Oxford: Clarendon, 1996).

Reich, *The Mass Psychology of Fascism* (1933; rpt. New York: Farrar, Straus & Giroux, 1970).

———, *The Sexual Revolution: Toward a Self-Regulating Character Structure*, trans. Therese Pol (New York: Farrar, Straus and Giroux, 1974).

———, *Character Analysis*, trans. V.R. Carfagno (New York: Farrer, Straus and Giroux, 1945).

Riesman, David, with Nathan Glazer and Reuek Denney, *The Lonely Crowd: A Study of the Changing American Character* (New Haven: Yale University Press, 1950).

Ringer, Fritz K. *The Decline of the German Mandarins: The German Academic Community, 1890–1933* (Cambridge, MA: Harvard University Press, 1969), 436.

Robinson, Paul A., *The Freudian Left: Wilhelm Reich, Géza Róheim, Herbert Marcuse* (New York: Harper Colophon Books, 1969), pp. 4–5.

Rosenbaum, Ron, *Explaining Hitler: The Search for the Origins of His Evil* (New York: De Capo Press, 2014)

Said, Edward, *Reflections on Exile and Other Essays* (Cambridge, MA: Harvard University Press, 2000).

Schaffner, Bertram Henry, *Father Land: A Study of Authoritarianism in the German Family* (New York: Columbia University Press, 1948).

Schor, Esther, *Bridge of Words: Esperanto and the Dream of a Universal Language* (New York: Metropolitan, 2016).

Schulin, Ernst, "German and American Historiography in the Nineteenth and Twentieth Centuries," in *Interrupted Past: German-Speaking Refugee Historians in the United States after 1933*, ed. Hartmut Lehmann and James J. Sheehan (Cambridge, UK: Cambridge University Press, 1991).

Shalit Erel, and Stein, M., eds. *Turbulent Times, Creative Minds: Erich Neumann and C. G. Jung in Relationship (1933–1960)*, eds. (Asheville, NC: Chiron, 2016).

Sharaf, Myron, *Fury on Earth: A Biography of Wilhelm Reich* (New York: St. Martin's Press, 1983).

Sterba, Richard, *Reminiscences of a Viennese Psychoanalyst* (Detroit: Wayne State University Press, 1982).

Strick, James E., *Wilhelm Reich, Biologist* (Cambridge, MA: Harvard University Press, 2015).

Tawney, Richard Henry, *Religion and the Rise of Capitalism: A Historical Study* (London: John Murray, 1926).

Young-Bruehl, Elizabeth, *Anna Freud: A Biography* (New Haven: Yale University Press, 2008).

Waite, Robert G. L., *The Psychological God: Adolf Hitler* (New York: Basic Books, 1977).

Weber, Max, *The Protestant Ethic and the Spirit of Capitalism*, trans. Talcott Parsons (1905; London: George Allen & Unwin, Ltd., 1930).

Weinstein, David, and Zakai, Avihu, *Jewish Exiles and European Thought in the Shadow of the Third Reich* (Cambridge, UK: Cambridge University Press, 2017).

Whitman, Walt, *Leaves of Grass*, ed. W. Blodgett and S. Bradley (New York: New York University Press, 1965).

Wittgenstein, Ludwig, *Vermischte Bemerkungen*, ed. Georg Henrik von Wright in collaboration with Heikki Neiman (Frankfurt am Main: Suhrkamp, 1977); *Culture and Value*, rev ed. Alois Pichler, trans. Peter Winch (London: Wiley-Blackwell, 1998).

Wood, E. Thomas, and Jankowski, Stanisław M. *Karski: How One Man Tried to Stop the Holocaust* (Hoboken: John Wiley & Sons, 1994).

Zakai, Avihu, *The Pen Confronts the Sword: Exiled German Scholars Challenge Nazism* (Albany: SUNY Press, 2018a).

———, *Erich Auerbach and the Crisis of German Philology: The Humanist Tradition in Peril* (Dordrecht: Springer, 2017).

———, "A Psychological Inquiry into Totalitarianism: Erich Fromm's *Escape from Freedom*," *Society*, 55, 5 (Fall 2018b): 440–50.

INDEX[1]

[1] Note: Page numbers followed by 'n' refer to notes.

A. Zakai, *Jewish Exiles' Psychological Interpretations of Nazism*,
https://doi.org/10.1007/978-3-030-54070-8

The manufacturer's authorised representative in the EU is Springer
Nature Customer Service Centre GmbH, Europaplatz 3, 69115 Heidelberg,
Germany. If you have any concerns regarding our products, please
contact ProductSafety@springernature.com

Printed and bound by CPI Group (UK) Ltd, Croydon, CR0 4YY
30/09/2026
02225514-0015